**breakfast,
lunch,
dinner,
life…**

recipes
and
adventures
from my
home
kitchen

**missy
robbins**

with
carrie king

photography by
evan sung

breakfast, lunch, dinner, life…

recipes and adventures from my home kitchen

missy robbins

with
carrie king

photography by
evan sung

introduction

I had a very fortunate upbringing. My parents were foodies before it was cool. Birthdays were spent traveling from suburban Connecticut into "the City" to go to the great restaurants of the day: The Four Seasons, Shun Lee Palace, Maxwell's Plum. I traveled to Israel, London, and Paris all before turning sixteen. At twelve, I dined at Le Gavroche in London, then a Michelin three-star restaurant. I can still recall every last morsel of food. Locally, big nights out in New Haven included dinner at our family's favorite red sauce joint, Leon's, a clubby establishment where my dad was known as "Doc" because we were such regulars. The table would always be filled with my parents' favorites, liver and fried sweetbreads—dishes that terrified me. While I was fascinated by the fanciness of restaurants, the pomp and circumstance of service and the buzz, I was a terrible eater. So picky. I had the nerve to select the most expensive dishes on the menu, like rack of lamb, and then ask for it well done. Fettuccine alfredo, but please hold any sign of green. Everything on a separate plate please, I don't like my vegetables to touch my meat. Oh, and no sauce please! Had I only known then what I know now. Still, I loved going to restaurants, from the local pizza joint to the most elegant places in Paris, because I loved food. It played a central role in our family.

When it comes to dining at home, my mother is a Jewish Martha Stewart. Every detail—from table settings to food—is impeccable within in the realm of the Carol Robbins' specialties. No matter the guest, she laid the table with our best china and vintage flatware. Floral centerpieces that she created herself were so beautiful that they could have just as easily been on display in a swank hotel or fancy restaurant. Her thoughtful touch extended beyond the dining room and throughout the house, even in the bathrooms, where guests were met with perfectly arranged soaps and fresh hand towels. In addition to the few delicious dishes that she cooked, her expertise in decor, proper entertaining, and hosting were branded in my brain from a very young age.

Never did I think any of this would lead to a career as a chef. Aside from a real reverence for food, I had a pretty traditional upbringing and education was a central piece. This meant a very competitive private high school followed by college at Georgetown. I never for a minute thought about going to culinary school. In my family, you went to college, period. It was 1989; there was no Food Network, and celebrity chefdom was a whole different animal. Cooking was an occupation and a craft, not a path to fame and fortune. It wasn't in the cards for me. If anything, from time to time I would dream that a successful career in some other field would let me open a restaurant for fun in retirement. Ha! What did I know? I was barely twenty!

I studied art history and psychology in college. I didn't feel pressured to be pre-med or pre-law or pre-anything because my parents believed that as long as you were studying something, honing your reading and analytical skills, you would be prepared for anything life throws your way. I interned at galleries and museums during my first three years at Georgetown, but never really found my calling. Becoming a therapist was a recurring thought, but not one I ever explored seriously.

It was an epic dinner at Charlie Trotter's in November 1992 that changed my path forever. My family and I were in Chicago visiting my grandmother for Thanksgiving, and to celebrate my brother's birthday we went to Trotter's. From the moment I sat down, the elegance of the glassware and flatware impeccably placed on the table impressed me. I was entranced by every detail of every dish's artistic presentation and composition; even the beautiful, pristine nature of each vegetable excited me. The attentive service didn't miss a beat, but at the same time was so non-intrusive that the servers were almost invisible. I had been in other high end restaurants before, but the combination of the magic I witnessed at Trotter's, and the right timing of my senior year, made something click inside me. That night I decided I wanted to cook and own a restaurant just like Trotter's. However, aside from some cooking at home, I had never properly held a knife!

I found out that I had a childhood friend that was apprenticing at Charlie Trotter's. She had gone to Northwestern and it opened my eyes to the fact that you could go to a top university and become a cook. I thought, well, if she can do it, so can I. After that memorable meal, I reached out to her to see how I could get hired. Frankly, she was not all that encouraging, stressing how difficult it would be for me to get in the door. Nonetheless, I wrote Chef Trotter a letter and sent my resume. This was before email was an acceptable way to apply for a job; there was no Craigslist. You sent a letter and you waited. Sure enough, three weeks later the phone rang and my roommate picked up—yelling that some guy named Charlie was on the phone. Oh shit! My nerves were instantly jumbled. I got on the phone and he grilled me. He told me to take a few days off of school and come spend time in his kitchen. That's exactly what I did and it was the most terrifying two days of my life; I had never been in a professional kitchen. The atmosphere was intense and serious. It seemed like everyone cooked in fear of making a mistake. But there was an inspiring energy that comes from the well-timed movements of a team in sync. I picked herbs. All day.

I left my two-day stint feeling hopeful in spite of my uncertainty as to whether I would have a home in Chicago after graduation. I was in the second semester of my senior year and really needed to figure out what I was going to do after graduation. Not working was not an option. My parents had been generous enough already in not making my brother and me have jobs while in college, so I had to figure it out. Charlie had suggested that I get some kitchen experience in D.C. while I finished school. This seemed crazy as I was much more focused on just showing up to class and going to The Tombs, the local bar. He suggested I work at The Watergate for Jean-Louis Palladin, a D.C. and international legend. Fearless and clueless, I dropped my resume off and a few days later he politely responded that he did not have room for me in his kitchen. Determined to get a cooking job, I went to 1789, the fancy restaurant above The Tombs. 1789 was where you took your parents when they visited D.C.; waiters were uniformed in tuxedos, the ambiance was dark and formal, old-school Washington with really excellent food. The dishes weren't particularly mind-blowing, but everything was tasty and simple and rooted in classic American cuisine. It was clearly a place where I could pick up the foundational cooking techniques I needed, like steaming mussels and making a true Caesar dressing. I knocked on the door and told the executive sous chef I wanted to work and learn and I'd do anything they needed. He told me to be there on Friday at 4:00 p.m. This was my first major restaurant lesson: weekends were no longer days off. I agreed, telling myself that the worst that could happen would be that I would hate it and quit. That was more than 1100 weekends ago.

That first Friday shift was amazing. The salad cook didn't show up and I was thrown right into the trenches. Wow! I was doing this. I loved everything about it: the energy, the smells, the food, the artistry, the order mixed in with the chaos. I never looked at my watch, didn't have a minute to be bored, and it seemed even on day one that I had the potential to be good at this thing called cooking (even though what I was really doing was mostly making cold plates and salads). I came back the next day, the next weekend, and the weekend after that. I was learning in a way that you don't learn in Philosophy 101. This was different. The people were different. The expectations were different. It was exhilarating.

After that first Friday shift, I was hooked and fully committed to pursuing a career in cooking. It was February 1993; I had just turned twenty-two and had three months until graduation. I went from having no plan to being eager to make seven dollars an

hour after graduating from one of the most prestigious universities in the country. Not quite what I would have imagined a few months earlier, and most likely not what my parents had in mind, but when I told them this was the plan and asked for their help financially, they were eagerly supportive. Charlie Trotter had never really given me a definitive answer on a job at his restaurant in Chicago and I loved my work at 1789. So I decided to stay at 1789 after graduation, without a notion of where it would lead. I was learning a lot and that's really all that mattered.

When you are in your twenties and cooking, life is pretty great. My only responsibility was to show up in the afternoon, set up my station, and put out great food throughout service. The fringe benefits are great for your social life. You get to wake up late, meet your friends out late. You're living in the moment and you don't realize that you're missing out on some aspects of life. Maybe, at times, not having weekends off was awkward and annoying, but it wasn't enough to really bother me. I was so engrossed in the learning process and trying to become an excellent cook that nothing else really mattered. I voluntarily showed up to assist the sous chefs on special projects. On my time off I read cookbooks like other people read novels. I ate new foods as much as possible. I did everything I could to eat, live, and breathe cooking.

This fast-paced, living-in-the-moment work blocks any awareness of what this life might mean for the years ahead. When you're in your twenties and full of energy and your joints are limber and most of your friends are staying up all hours anyway, time goes by fast and everything seems light. You can't really prepare yourself for the toll this profession eventually takes.

All of the sudden, twenty years had passed. I'd moved up the chain. With Executive Chef scrawled on the breast of my coat, I felt like I'd finally achieved the mastery over my craft that I had strived for since my first days at Trotter's. With that, I had been lucky to receive some critical acclaim and recognition from my chef peers and it all seemed to be happening just as I had dreamed. But my hours had increased, my responsibility had increased, and the twelve-to-fourteen hour workdays had taken a toll emotionally and physically. I was often absent at family occasions, and when I did get to attend events, I would be so tired that it was sometimes challenging to be fully engaged and all I could think about was catching up on much-needed sleep. It was difficult to keep up with friends and schedule dinners and brunches. I realized that I almost always felt torn, as if I were being pulled in many directions. And then there was the physical aspect. While cooking professionally does keep you strong and active, I'd developed joint problems, shoulder issues, back issues, and suffered from a general lack of taking care of myself.

I have always cherished the positives of becoming a chef: the food, learning, camaraderie, "cool" factor, fast-paced restaurant buzz, lack of normalcy, not planting myself at a desk everyday. And maybe I focused on those things too much because I ignored the fact that all this lack of normalcy didn't always make me happy. I had a consciousness of it at times that would sometimes creep into the forefront of my mind, but the tough girl in me always had the drive to push harder and succeed more.

But what does success mean if you don't have the time or energy to enjoy it? If you work 100 hours in six days? If you are too tired to really take advantage of your one day off, or maybe two in a good week? At some point, it became clear that it was time for me to reassess. I just needed to clear my head, and then really figure out what might make me truly happy at this point in my life. So, in May 2013, when I left A Voce, it wasn't just a sense that I needed to leave my current job for a different one. It was that I didn't even know if restaurants and cooking were the right answers anymore. To that point in my career, I had been lucky enough to never experience earth-shattering

Napoli in bocca

≡ Sicilia e le isole in bocca ≡

≡ Sardegna in bocca ≡

≡ Liguria in bocca ≡

Le Conserve della Nonne

1979
"il Vespro"

disappointment or major rejection, which left me fueled with the confidence that I had to land on my feet . . . eventually. This might explain why when so many people seemed incredulous that I was leaving A Voce with no real plan, I didn't necessarily see it as the giant leap that everyone else did. It felt like the move that I had to make and I believed, perhaps naively in hindsight, that everything would work out somehow. I just had no idea what that picture would look like. One moment I would think that maybe cooking was right after all, but I needed to start my own business to be happy. That thought would mull around in my mind for a while before it would lead me to the idea that what I really needed was to leave food altogether and go back to school. But what would I go back to school for? It was clear that I was unclear. There were many questions to answer and I knew I could not find those answers without making a clean break. Though possibly insane to take the risk and have no plan and no income in a crazy expensive city like New York, I didn't see any alternative to taking a leap of faith. I had been on autopilot for the better part of the last twenty years, making choices to submerge myself deeper and deeper in the restaurant industry. While I never intended for these questions to take so long to answer, I knew I needed time to figure out my next adventure.

the art of grocery shopping

When I was a kid I loved going to the grocery store with my mom. It brought me great joy to roam through each aisle as we searched for our old standbys for the pantry: the perfect potato chip, Temp Tee whipped cream cheese, Doritos, salsa, Cracker Barrel cheddar cheese, French dressing. My palate was not as sophisticated as it is now, but I think what excited me was the sheer variety. Instead of a kid in a candy store, I was a kid in a grocery store. But for the suburbs, my family had a unique approach to shopping because it wasn't just one-stop shopping at the grocery store. My mother rounded out our "regular" grocery store haul with meat from the kosher butcher, fish from the fish market, a stop at the Italian market for oils, cheeses, and olives, the cheese shop for fancy cheeses, the farm stand and orchard for apples, and so on. As I got older, I found it to be a pain in the ass that we spent so much time in the car running from place to place. In and out of the car. In and out of the car. But, like any great chef that values the quality of ingredients, my mom knew where the best was and she wouldn't settle for less. The multiple stops for hours on end drove me insane, but once in the stores my eyes were always wide open and I loved assessing the "product." It was so important—the right piece of salmon, the right piece of Brie (there was a lot of Boursin purchased as well), the right cut of brisket, the right kosher hot dog . . . This type of shopping and scrutiny was ingrained in me at an early age, and being so attracted to the process paved the way for me to become a chef.

When I actually started cooking professionally, I never ate at home. I never kept food in the house, except for maybe a few staples like olive oil and pasta. I didn't need to. For one, I had terrible eating habits and never ate until I got to work. And two, I always worked and didn't have time to eat at home. On my days off the last thing I wanted to do was cook. I wanted to try other restaurants and absorb what was happening in whatever city I called home. The meandering grocery shopping I once loved became a foreign concept. I got what I needed in quick spurts on demand, usually at a bodega or corner store or whatever spot was easiest. For twenty years, every time I had the occasion to cook at home, I had to start from scratch and get everything I needed, from eggs to olive oil (which had usually gone rancid sitting on the shelf, unused in the months since I last cooked).

When I left my job and tried to live like a somewhat normal civilian, I quickly discovered that I had strange food shopping habits. I would crave yogurt for breakfast, so I would go out and buy one yogurt. Later on, I'd get hungry for lunch and go out again to grab romaine to make a salad. Dinner would roll around and I'd want pasta, so out I went again. As a chef in a restaurant, we are used to having everything at our fingertips. You don't think about needing anything because you have a very deep, constantly restocked pantry, full of every spice, condiment, oil, cheese, nut, flour, and any other dry good you can imagine. When hunger strikes at work, you do a tour of the walk-in fridge for inspiration and make something on a whim. It's second nature. We don't have to think. We just cook. And during my time off, it struck me that that's what you should be able to do at home, too. And that most people, other than crazy chefs like me, probably do.

Fixing my pantry wasn't that big of a hurdle, once I decided to stock it. The larger problem is that I never know what I want to eat in a given moment. I'm driven by cravings and ingredient inspiration—I'm just not a meal planner. But, having the basics around—spices, oils, salt, vinegars, dried pastas, all the stuff that won't go bad—makes life easier. Now that I've rediscovered my love for grocery shopping, I find I have returned to the habits instilled by my mom. I rarely go to a big grocery store. I still like to go to the Italian market, the cheese shop, the fish market, the butcher (though definitely not the kosher one), and most importantly, the farmers market. Now that I'm a New Yorker who walks everywhere and not a teenage kid being dragged around in the suburbs, I do have much more appreciation for the car because the alternative— schlepping tons of heavy bags around for blocks—gets pretty old.

I've put together a guide to all the ingredients I now make sure to always have in my home pantry and fridge. Knowing these ingredients are on hand doesn't curtail my creativity; instead, it allows me to make the spontaneous choices that I think are the most fun part of cooking. You won't have to get far into this book to learn what my most essential ingredients are (garlic, olive oil, lemons, chili flakes). I have only included the items that are on heavy rotation in my home kitchen and that I would feel lost without.

building the pantry

anchovies Many people tell me that they are scared of anchovies, but used properly and sparingly, they can add just the right amount of umami to a dish. And as you'll see in this book, I also enjoy them as the star of the show. Italian or Spanish varieties found in specialty markets are a step beyond, but the most common brand, Roland, does the job just fine.

anchovy paste Anchovy paste doesn't have the same quality as whole anchovies, but is great to have in the pantry when you're in a rush or are out of the whole ones.

balsamic vinegar The world of balsamic vinegar is huge. I very rarely use generic balsamic, and prefer one with a bit more age. My go-to for many years has been Villa Manodori, produced by the esteemed Italian chef Massimo Bottura. It is thick, just sweet enough, and has all the grape notes important to balsamic with a hint of acid. Balsamic is a place to splurge if you can. For the quality, his is reasonably priced—and a little goes a long way.

basil Adds freshness to any dish. Even though you can get it all year round, it's definitely superior when in season.

beans I use mostly canned beans at home to save time. There are plenty of good, organic brands available.

black peppercorns You will see throughout the book that I use a pepper mill to grind fresh pepper wherever it is needed. This makes a big difference—never buy ground pepper.

capers Always buy capers packed in salt. Your food will benefit more from their inherent salty flavor than their brine-packed counterparts that taste too pickled. (Salt-packed capers need to be soaked in water for 30 to 60 minutes before use.)

chili flakes Basic and simple, but offers an intense heat.

citrus [lemons & oranges] I use citrus in most everything I cook; the juice and, probably more prominently, the zest. The oils from the peels pack a huge punch of flavor that brightens just about any dish. I'm addicted. Make sure to remove any white pith while using zest or you will have very bitter results.

coarse sea salt For finishing dishes.

coriander seeds Brings an earthy, citrusy note. Love to use it just freshly cracked for added texture and a pop of bright flavor.

crushed calabrian chiles Tutto Calabria makes a wide range of products and is the only brand that is readily available in Italian specialty stores and online. My favorite is their crushed hot chili peppers; they are VERY spicy so a little goes a long way. I also like that you get the added bonus of the chili oil, which can be drizzled on pizza, fish, vegetables, and pasta.

dried pasta I am a simple girl. I like De Cecco. Most people are shocked by this because it is a common brand that you can find in almost every supermarket, but it's got great texture, which is the most important thing. If you want to go a little fancier and artisanal with dried pasta, my pick is Rustichella d'Abruzzo.

fennel It's in a lot of recipes in the book, but frankly I just like to keep it around to eat raw because it's a great, healthy snack.

fennel pollen I call this my "magic dust" because it has a way of making everything taste amazing; it is a great finisher to vegetables, meat, fish, and poultry. While it is not cheap (it's generally hand harvested from the fennel flower) it's worth every penny and you don't need much of it to make an impact.

fennel seeds I think I use this in ninety-nine percent of my dishes. It's assertive, but never overwhelming.

flat-leaf italian parsley Whenever I refer to parsley, it always means flat-leaf Italian. Curly parsley does not exist in my world.

garlic I think fresh garlic is likely my most used ingredient: roasted, sliced, chopped, whole cloves, whole heads. You will see throughout the book that it takes on different characteristics depending on how you use it.

garlic powder It might be surprising that a chef would love garlic powder as much as I do. I also like to use it in addition to fresh garlic for a second dimension of garlic flavor.

honey A great alternative to refined sugar.

kosher salt Diamond Kosher is my brand of choice. I prefer the texture over other salts and it is my go-to salt for all-around seasoning. You will become very good friends with salt over the course of this book.

marjoram I like to refer to marjoram as the feminine version of oregano.

olive oil This is one of the most important ingredients in any pantry. Always buy 100% extra-virgin as it is the purest form of olive oil. There are many, many differences in quality and flavor across brands and even production regions, so you'll have to do some experimenting to find ones that suit your needs and palate. Generally, you want one that is balanced in flavor to use as your cooking oil for everyday use, and one with a little more nuance for finishing dishes. I tend to favor oils with milder, grassy notes for fish, and a more buttery, peppery finish for meat.

parmigiano-reggiano This cheese reigns supreme in northern Italy. It is a bit nuttier than its southern sibling, Pecorino, but still salty. Terrific on its own and grated over pastas, meats, and vegetables.

pecorino romano I can't live without Pecorino.

pink peppercorns I have a special love for the underutilized pink peppercorn. They are floral and sweet and intense. Use sparingly.

red wine vinegar My workhorse vinegar. Not all red wine vinegars are created equal; my preferred brand is one from Italy called Trucialetto. Red wine vinegar is a place to spend a little extra money to get better quality because you want something with decent body, but also a deeper balance of flavor that doesn't just taste like acid.

rosemary Be careful not to use too much because it can be medicinal in taste, so it's best to add it towards the end of cooking.

san marzano tomatoes San Marzano tomatoes are only truly San Marzano tomatoes if they come from that place in Italy. After many years of tasting and testing, I always use La Valle brand. They are consistent in flavor and have the perfect balance of acidity and sweetness.

tomato passato If you want to make a quick sauce and don't want to deal with cans and hand-crushing tomatoes, passato is great to have because the work has already been done for you.

thyme Always use fresh thyme, never dried.

other necessities Dijon and grainy mustard, onions, tomato paste, hot paprika, smoked paprika, sweet paprika, hot sauce.

oh shit, what have i done

Before I left A Voce, normally I would hit snooze until the very last minute that still allowed me to scramble out of bed, get dressed, grab a cup of coffee at Joe, and end up running into work at 10:14 on the dot. "Normally" was six days a week for most of the last five years.

Truthfully, my first jobless day didn't feel all that out of the ordinary because it was a Sunday, which had been my usual day off from work. But, after a couple of days I found myself lying in bed with nowhere to be except Pilates. No excuses for my poor habit of not eating breakfast (or lunch, for that matter). No reason to chug my large latte. No real grounds for getting out of bed at all, other than when I had plans with friends. And while I had been looking forward to this moment with great anticipation for the last six months, I soon realized that nothing can really prepare you for the simultaneous feelings of elation and sudden purposelessness.

I figured I had one opportunity in my career to take a sabbatical of sorts, so I felt like I used that get-out-of-jail-free card the day I turned in my notice. It wasn't a decision I took lightly—I thought long and hard about it and had no regrets. I also had no plans. None at all. I had no idea what the hell I was going to do with myself. I just knew I needed a change. It's not like I was looking for an *Eat, Pray, Love* moment exactly—I just wanted a break. I didn't even consciously feel burned out, though it wasn't long before it became obvious that I had been. I remember having to do press before my departure from A Voce and one particular interview with Florence Fabricant from the *New York Times* stands out in my mind. She kept pressing me for my next moves, which wasn't surprising. It seemed like every chef and food journalist I knew was wondering what I would do next. Everyone believed there had to be a big secret project I was moving on to. I kept telling her, as I told everyone, I had no plans. Really. After enough pressure, I finally caved and told her that I was taking time off to travel and write a book—neither of which was totally true, but I supposed not entirely out of the question either. I told her that because I felt like I had to have a better answer than the real truth: I needed time for myself.

It was totally out of character for me to just leave a prestigious job for time off. I frankly have no idea what gave me the notion or nerve to make such an uncharacteristic and risky decision. Any time I had left a job in the past it was to go straight into a different position, one that would advance my career. This was different because from the outside it may have seemed irrational, but in my gut it felt right. And so, defying conventional wisdom, I left a dream job for no job. Free to spend the day lazing in my sweatpants, pondering life while slowly sipping my latte. And so it began.

I didn't plan to have the beginning of my year off coincide with the end of spring and beginning of summer. In fact, at that time, I didn't really even know that I would be gifting myself an entire year. It was just supposed to be an indefinite amount of time to myself. But, given the timing and the weather, it didn't take long for me to adjust. After a couple of days, I was happily planning my own personal adult summer camp. My days were soon filled with coffee and lunch dates, shopping for shoes a woman on a budget shouldn't have been buying, wandering the streets of the West Village, indulging in long dinners with friends, drinking Aperol spritzes and negronis on a whim, taking my time at the gym. It was the first time since college that I had a legitimate social life. I no longer had to study a calendar or consult a schedule to find a *possible* week where I *might* be free in the next few months to get together. I'm not saying that I have that many friends; it was just amazing to be able to freely catch up with the ones that I do have. I tried to love every minute of it, constantly reminding myself to enjoy the moment while also living in secret fear that the bliss of the honeymoon period would disappear and give way to stress and worry. It seemed inevitable. It is one thing to enjoy an indulgent week or two off between jobs. It is another thing when you have an ocean of time off with no new job in sight, and the guilt that comes with spending and eating out. It's not like I had a rich spouse or a trust fund waiting in the wings. Still, I stood my ground and committed to staying unemployed for the summer, which considering my phone started to ring within days of my freedom, wasn't easy. I was a free agent and headhunters were on the prowl. Realtors wanted to know whether I was looking for a restaurant space, when all I was looking for was peace and quiet. Oddly, while at A Voce, I very rarely received calls from potential partners or employers trying to woo me away. I think people assumed I was extremely committed to the restaurant, which I was, and just had the respect not to approach me or tempt me to leave. But now it was different and I was different. I politely declined conversations and potential job offers remaining firm and clear that I wasn't looking for employment, while not giving potentially valuable contacts the idea that I was brushing them off. Perhaps a mistake because eventually my phone stopped ringing. Well now what? I got slightly worried. It's not like I never wanted to work again, I just wanted a few months off.

Week one was liberating and terrifying for that very reason. What if I never figured out what I wanted to do next? I was 42 years old, why didn't I already have this figured out? I had always thought I would have owned my own place by then; did that mean I was a failure? Was I better off just biting the bullet and opening my own little pasta shop and market? Or was I better off not owning my own place at all? Did everyone think I was insane? The questions and uncertainties and contradictions swirled around in my brain incessantly. It is fair to say I was a little lost.

But as week one turned into week two, and month three bled into month four, I found I had settled into this new lifestyle and really enjoyed it. I still had my doubts and moments of uncertainty, and maybe the answer to the question was, *Yes, everyone does think you are insane*. But, at that moment it didn't matter because I was quite happy relishing sweaty summer days in New York City, sitting at cafés, taking in the bounty of the greenmarkets, going to Montauk, and generally relishing the newfound and totally foreign feeling of pure freedom. I trusted the questions would get answered eventually. Right?

breakfast

Growing up, the same thing happened every single morning. I would wake up, shower, come downstairs to get out the door for school and, without fail, I would hear my mother's voice, *Can I get you breakfast? What do you want to eat? Cereal? Fruit? Eggs? Oatmeal?* And, every morning for 17 years, I said, *Nothing, I'm fine,* before disappearing.

This unavoidable early morning exchange used to drive me insane. My answer never changed. I never wanted breakfast, but this never prevented my mother from offering a rundown of all the options. But it turns out that mothers really do know best because when I started my quest to be healthy during my time off, I learned that eating breakfast was kind of required if I wanted to successfully lose weight and balance my appetite so that I wasn't gorging later in the day. Now it's become so ingrained into my morning routine that if I don't eat breakfast, I end up angry, hungry, and prone to an afternoon binge on whatever happens to be in front of me.

But although I recognize the benefits of eating breakfast now, it was definitely a challenge to integrate into my life. A somewhat healthy breakfast that isn't just sugary cereal or granola requires a certain amount of thought and effort and groceries in the house, and in the morning, it can be hard to motivate into prep mode. For the most part, I keep breakfast simple, but flavorful; and as in most of my cooking, I try to elevate the ordinary to extraordinary without having to make it a two-hour process. So, these are all recipes that are easy to prepare and can be made quickly. Some are healthier than others, but most importantly they all taste delicious and are dishes that get me ready to go, but that also keep me fueled for a good part of the day.

winter citrus, pistachios, mint

serves 4

I am a fanatic about citrus. I even like to eat lemons and limes. I know. It's weird. When winter is dark, vegetables are brown, and seasonal fresh greens are sparse, citrus peaks and sheds a little light on the winter doldrums. I think that most people just associate citrus with sour, but with so many varieties combined in this dish, you can truly appreciate the nuanced flavor that each brings—sweet, sour, tart, and bitter. Pistachios add crunch while mint adds dimension. If you want to make this a more savory dish, add a drizzle of olive oil and a sprinkle of sea salt.

4	Meyer lemons
4	ruby red grapefruits
4	blood oranges
4	tangerines
4	navel oranges
4 tablespoons	unsalted pistachios, roughly chopped
2	sprigs mint, leaves only

1   Zest the lemons and reserve the zest. Use a paring knife to cut away the skin and pith from each piece of fruit.
2   Over a large bowl, segment each piece of citrus, making sure to remove any seeds and squeezing their juices into the bowl. Toss lightly.
3   Evenly divide the fruit among four bowls, making sure to get a little of each type of citrus and juice into each bowl. Top with the pistachios, mint, and reserved lemon zest.

hazelnut yogurt, dried figs, cocoa
serves 4

Possibly one of the best things I ate during my stay in Alba while in Piemonte on my year off was hazelnut yogurt. It was not from an artisan company or specially homemade (it was packaged rather commercially from a German company). But it was delicious. Nut yogurts are not something we see often in the States and it was revelatory to me. Nutty, earthy, tangy, and slightly sweet. When I came home I looked high and low for it and couldn't find it anywhere, so I came up with this recreation of the magical breakfast treat. If you're not using it all right away, store the yogurt in a tightly sealed container in the fridge to enjoy all week.

1 quart	Greek yogurt
2 cups	skinless hazelnuts, toasted until golden brown, plus 4 tablespoons for garnish
2 tablespoons	hazelnut oil
¼ cup	honey
4–8	dried figs, cut in ¼-inch slices
1 tablespoon	cocoa powder

1 Place the yogurt in a blender and with the blender on high speed. Gradually add the nuts, stopping occasionally to scrape down the sides. Continue blending until the nuts are fully incorporated and the mixture is smooth.
2 With the blender still on, gradually pour in the hazelnut oil.
3 Mix in the honey.
4 To serve, divide the yogurt into four bowls. Evenly distribute the figs around the top, followed by the hazelnuts. Finish with a dusting of cocoa powder.

hazelnut yogurt, dried figs, cocoa
pg 25

summer stone fruits, yogurt, coriander honey
pg 28

summer stone fruits, yogurt, coriander honey

serves 4

I love a simple breakfast of yogurt and fruit because it fills me up, has lots of protein, and I feel good about starting my day off with something healthy. I prefer savory breakfasts to sweet ones, so I added coriander to the honey, which adds a nutty, earthy, citrusy note, plus texture from the roughly cracked seeds. The longer you let the honey and coriander sit together, the better. You can even make a larger batch to use as an accompaniment to fresh cheeses, like ricotta or goat, or with other fruit combinations.

1½ tablespoons	coriander seeds
4 tablespoons	honey
3 cups	Greek yogurt
8	whole stone fruits, assorted, pitted, and cut into ½-inch wedges

1 Spread the coriander seeds on a cutting board and, using the back of a heavy sauté pan, crush the seeds until they split in half.
2 In a small bowl, combine the split seeds and honey.
3 To serve, evenly divide the yogurt among four bowls, distribute the sliced fruits on top, and finish with a drizzle of the coriander honey.

oatmeal with saba and raspberries

serves 4

In the past, the only oatmeal I knew was loaded with cream, milk, sugar, and butter, sort of defeating the point of a healthy breakfast and moving straight into basically eating dessert in the morning. But oatmeal was an ideal choice when I first got hooked on my newfound breakfast habit, because it kept me full for hours, so I had to figure out how to make oatmeal cooked with water (instead of deliciously rich dairy) taste good without adding a ton of sugar, fat, and calories. I started adding berries towards the end of cooking and finishing with *saba*, a condiment of cooked grape must popular in Italy. It adds sweetness and depth to the dish, with an Italian touch. Fresh berries at their peak are obviously delicious, but when not in season good quality frozen berries yield a great result. In fact, I started to prefer the frozen ones because I could keep them on hand and they actually break down nicely when cooked in this dish. If you have the time needed to prepare traditional steel cut oats, great, but I am a fan of McCann's quick-cooking steel-cut oats for efficiency, which on most days, is a must.

4 cups	water
2 cups	McCann's quick-cooking rolled oats
2 cups	fresh or frozen raspberries
	pinch of kosher salt
	saba, for drizzling

1 Bring water to a boil and add the oatmeal. Stir and cook for 3 minutes.
2 Add the berries and the salt and cook for another 2 minutes, continuing to stir. The berries will break down slightly into the oatmeal.
3 Divide between 4 bowls, drizzle with the *saba*.

soft scrambled eggs, smoked sable, crème fraîche, caviar

serves 4

This indulgent, luxurious breakfast came about from leftovers I had after a Russ & Daughters brunch that, as always, included several different types of smoked fish, caviar, and other treats. I'm a fan of treating oneself to the best wherever you can get it and see no reason to reserve good ingredients like caviar or smoked fish for special occasions. I only like scrambled eggs when they are soft and creamy and this recipe will teach you how to get there every time. The key is patience. Feel free to sub the sable for smoked trout or salmon or whatever fish you like if sable is not available. Also, I use American caviar; it is less expensive but still gives the same salty, briny sensation with a pop of texture.

2 teaspoons	butter
8	eggs, beaten
2 tablespoons	crème fraîche
¼ teaspoon	kosher salt
4	large slices of smoked sable
1 ounce	caviar

1 Heat a medium saucepan over low heat. Add the butter and melt.
2 Add the eggs and stir with a wooden spatula, being sure to occasionally scrape down the sides of the pan.
3 Continue stirring on low heat, for about 5 minutes, until eggs are just cooked. They should look creamy, just set, and without any brown color.
4 Remove the pan from the heat and stir in the crème fraîche.
5 Season with a touch of salt, but not too much because the fish and caviar will also add some salt and briny flavor.
6 To serve, divide the eggs among four plates, topping each with a piece of sable and one-quarter of the caviar.

fried egg with kasha, sicilian pesto, and soppressata

serves 4

My Polish grandmother is most likely rolling over in her grave knowing that I now combine kasha, which she served during my childhood Varnishkes style with bow-tie pasta and onions (one of my very favorite dishes), with cured pork. I have always loved the nutty flavor of kasha, or buckwheat, and it also has the added bonus of being both gluten- and wheat-free. When combined with a fried egg and the tanginess of sundried tomatoes and peppers, along with spicy *soppressata*, the result is a truly savory and energizing, protein- and fiber-packed meal to start the day off right. In fact, it's so robust that it would make a great lunch and even dinner. By the way, there is no such thing as Sicilian pesto … I made it up. The sauce is made from typically Sicilian ingredients and the name sounded fitting, so now it's stuck.

for the kasha

2 cups water
1 tablespoon kosher salt
1 cup kasha

1   Bring the water to a boil, add the salt and kasha, and bring the heat down to a very low simmer.
2   Cook, covered, for approximately 15 minutes, until the water is absorbed. Turn off the heat, but keep the kasha covered, allowing it to finish steaming for another 5–10 minutes until it is tender, but not mushy.
3   Fluff with a fork and set aside.

for the sicilian pesto

2 cups finely chopped sundried tomatoes
1 cup finely chopped sundried peppers
5 garlic cloves, finely chopped
1 cup finely chopped spicy soppressata
zest of 2 oranges
3 cups olive oil
2–3 tablespoons Calabrian chili oil (from a jar of Calabrian chiles)

1   Combine the tomatoes, peppers, garlic, soppressata, and orange zest in a bowl.
2   Add the olive and chili oils and mix. The mixture should be just combined, not too liquidy. The pesto will be best after it sits for a few hours or days so that the flavors combine and will keep in a tightly sealed container in the refrigerator, covered by the oil for a few weeks. It also can be used as a dressing for vegetables.

for the finish

¾ cup	Sicilian pesto
	juice of half an orange
1 tablespoon	red wine vinegar
1 tablespoon	olive oil
4	large eggs
2½ cups	cooked kasha

1. Place the pesto in a bowl and stir in the orange juice along with the red wine vinegar. The acid will brighten up the flavors.
2. Heat a large non-stick pan over medium heat and add the olive oil.
3. Crack the eggs into the pan and cook sunny side up until the whites have set.
4. To serve, divide the kasha among four bowls and place one egg on top, finished with some of the Sicilian pesto.

fried egg with kasha, tickling pesto and soppressata
pg 30

eggs in purgatorio
pg 34

eggs in purgatorio

serves 4

For me, this spicy tomato "purgatory" is really heaven. It has been my go-to egg dish for years because I get to eat eggs, which I don't usually love, masked by all the flavors of a great pasta, which clearly is what I would really like to be eating. And it's another great use for the Arrabbiata sauce on page 112. This dish is very savory and makes for a filling breakfast, and is also hearty enough for lunch. Use toasted country bread to sop up all the sauce and runny yolks.

1 quart	Arrabbiata sauce
8	eggs
2 tablespoons	olive oil
1 teaspoon	chili flakes
1	sprig rosemary, leaves picked
½ cup	grated Pecorino Romano

1   Heat the Arrabbiata sauce in a large shallow pan over medium-low heat. If it is a little thick, thin it out with a bit of water.
2   Once the sauce is hot, gently crack the eggs, one by one, directly into the pan, making sure to spread them out so they are not on top of each other, but in one even layer scattered throughout the sauce.
3   Cover the pan and cook gently on medium-low heat until the egg whites set and the yolks are still runny, approximately 3–5 minutes.
4   Use a slotted spoon or spider to transfer the eggs to four bowls for serving, 2 eggs per person. Surround the eggs with the Arriabbiata sauce.
5   Garnish equally with the olive oil, chili flakes, rosemary leaves, and Pecorino.

zucchini and provolone frittata
serves 6–8

The key to a good frittata is the egg / vegetable / cheese ratio. I find most frittatas too eggy and without enough filling, which is the most interesting part. Frittatas should also be fairly flat and not too airy, another reason why the eggs should really just serve as a binder for the rest of the ingredients. I use both regular and sharp provolone here; regular gives the texture and the sharp adds the bite. The sweet zucchini coupled with the sharp provolone strikes the perfect balance.

5 cups	grated zucchini (about 3 medium)
2 tablespoons	olive oil
10	eggs, cracked and beaten
2 teaspoons	kosher salt
½ cup	grated provolone
¼ cup	grated sharp provolone

1. Preheat the oven to 375°F.
2. On the largest side of a box grater, grate the zucchini. Place the grated zucchini in the center of a clean kitchen towel, wrap it up and squeeze the water out. Set aside.
3. Place a large nonstick skillet over medium heat and add the olive oil.
4. Add the zucchini and stir, just to slightly sauté.
5. Add the eggs and salt, and stir to incorporate.
6. Add both cheeses and stir to distribute throughout the frittata, ensuring that the mixture is in one even layer in the pan. Cook on low heat until the eggs just begin to set, about 2–3 minutes.
7. Transfer the pan to the oven to finish cooking, about 8–10 minutes.
8. Once cooked, gently slide the frittata from the pan onto a platter. Cut into slices and serve.

adventures in my tiny kitchen

I remember the moment I found my apartment. I had been flying back and forth between Chicago and New York for months getting ready for the ultimate flight that would take me back to the big city after my five-year hiatus in the so-called second city. The West Village was always the goal, but increasingly seemed an unattainable one. It's expensive, and attractive apartments are small and few and far between. And yet I still wanted to be there. My realtor, also a good friend, had patiently shown me fifteen apartments throughout downtown NYC. There were spaces that were fine and maybe would have sufficed, and then there were spaces that were awesome but not in the right location, or over my budget. My now well-worn, but much-loved, West Village enclave was the last apartment I saw on a day of exhaustive looking. I was looking for a home. Somewhere that moved me. Charm. Warmth.

It was "the one." I knew it the minute I walked into its long, narrow hallway, down to a decently sized bedroom, a foyer and a modest, but charming, living room with a true working (sort of) fireplace all lit up with sunshine. The current tenant was a pack rat so the space was cluttered with not-so-attractive furniture and a cat. It was painted a pallid yellow and the beautiful fireplace was framed by a pair of ugly brass sconces, all topped off with a very dated, very ugly, also brass, chandelier. But I had a vision of what it could be. I would paint it bright white. My modern furniture would transform the space with its clean lines. I would change the lighting to bring it out of the Dark Ages. I would add bookcases and make my extensive cookbook collection a focal point. I was so enthralled with the location and the great light streaming in through the vintage casement windows, that I didn't give any thought to the kitchen and bathroom. This is how it goes in New York City. You find yourself looking past what would otherwise be deal-breakers because you are so beaten down by the search and are so elated to have finally found an apartment in your budget that isn't a hovel. When I did think about it, I realized that the bathroom was tiny. It had a stall shower barely big enough to bend your elbows and the toilet sat within inches of the sink. But: The light! The windows! The fireplace! The prime West Village location! I could live with it.

The kitchen should have been where I drew the line, but I didn't. Less than two feet of space between the stove and makeshift drop-down 14-inch counter behind it if you are facing the range. Literally no other counter space. No dishwasher. A narrow refrigerator. Only one pair of outlets, situated in a completely inconvenient location. There was however, a giant window. Years later, I am more willing to acknowledge that a window doesn't clean dishes, or give you space to rest a hot pan coming off the burner. But it looked pretty, with a view right onto the giant tree-lined block. It was like being in the country with all that visible greenery. Almost.

Could a chef live in a place with such a measly kitchen? The funny thing about chefs is that we are never home. Before this place, I rarely cooked in my apartment. After a ninety-hour work week I never had much interest in preparing a meal at home for myself. So, my home kitchen had always been sort of irrelevant; when I had time off, I wanted to be out eating someone else's food. At the time, I was about to start a job where, within a year, I would have not one, but two beautiful restaurant kitchens, both more than adequate to prepare anything my mind could ever dream up. At home, I basically needed a refrigerator to keep milk for cereal and bubbly wine for the occasional celebratory tipple. I needed a pot to make a hasty dinner of buttered pasta. I needed an oven to heat up the remnant leftovers of takeout baked ziti and eggplant parm. That's it. This is the life of a chef. A sort of sad reality when it's all laid out in front of you, and certainly not a normal existence. And since I grew up in a home where life revolved around the kitchen island, and where meals were lovingly cooked and then eaten together at the kitchen table, it was a strange one for me, even after twenty years of being in the business.

Little did I know when I looked past all of the shortcomings of this tiny kitchen that I would ever leave my job and turn into an active home cook. Even when I knew my days at A Voce were numbered, visions of life without a job looked like a lot of dining out. In those dreamy visions I conveniently neglected the financial implications of eating out every night. I wasn't considering the effect on my health that ordering in three to four times a week might have. I didn't think about needing to eat breakfast and lunch. I had always done that at work. Coffee on the way, a bowl of yogurt when I got there, and snacking on whatever was at my fingertips throughout the day.

Fast forward through five years of easily avoiding the task of having to do much real home cooking. I am now gainfully unemployed, and finally having to reckon with my tiny, ill-equipped, awkward kitchen. But I was a pro. I could make this happen. With a slight change in attitude, what started out as incredibly annoying, quickly turned into a kind of enjoyable series of challenges: How do I make a great meal using the least amount of pots and pans? How do I make pasta using the same pot to boil the pasta AND cook the sauce? How do I use the oven so that I never have to clean the stove? Where do I do knife work with such little counter space? Where do I wash vegetables if my sink is covered with a cutting board? Where do I store the silverware when someone builds a kitchen without drawers?

What I discovered is that it all can be done. It might look a little strange, or require some juggling and creativity—like laying a towel on the floor outside the kitchen to dry dishes—but I found myself using the principles of restaurant cooking and efficiency, just downsized a little. It was like having a station in a small basement New York City kitchen like the ones I started in. In both scenarios I had a two-foot space in which to work, and called on my Tetris skills to carve out just the right amount of space to fit one more thing in the fridge.

As my time off went on, cooking healthfully became a priority, and my bank account was steadily depleting at a rate faster than I foresaw. The result of both was that my kitchen became increasingly valuable to me. It also became a place of respite, infusing a sense of home where mellow dinners were made and quietly enjoyed away from the outside hustle of Manhattan life. Aside from the tips and tricks of using a small space, I learned to truly simplify food. I started using fewer ingredients and maximized their flavor. I learned that, unlike restaurant life, in home cooking if something is not perfect it's actually OK. Often I was cooking for one. Who would see my mistakes? I only had to make it taste great—or good enough—for me. But I still secretly always tried to make it pretty, too. This was cooking without human dishwashers to clean up after me and without prep cooks to peel my fava beans and potatoes. This was back-to-basics cooking in a tight space. I knocked shit over all the time, and I got pissed. But I was making delicious food. That's all that mattered. It's not the size of the kitchen; it's how you organize the space. How you prepare before cooking and gather your *mise en place*. The biggest upside: I was the only critic.

vegetables

As a kid, I was never a fan. I didn't like salad. Green things could not touch my plate. That's not entirely true—I liked cucumbers. Plain. And bell peppers.

For most of my adult life, while I didn't have quite the same disdain for vegetables, they never featured heavily in my own eating habits, even though I had grown to love cooking with them in my restaurants. I never craved vegetables. I didn't feel like they could fill me up. It was not until I changed my diet dramatically that I needed to make vegetables my best friend in the kitchen. If my eight-year-old self could see me now. I went from a pizza-, carb-, and meat-fueled world to cherishing every vegetable I could get my hands on. I challenged myself to make them taste as good as a bowl of pasta with butter and cheese. I started to push the envelope with technique and flavor combinations, but with a very simple and easy approach that doesn't *always* include piling on a lot of cheese. What I learned, aside from how much I adore vegetables, is that working with them brings out a different type of creativity that I love.

Instead of just providing sustenance, vegetables of all kinds became something I looked forward to, that I wanted to explore, and that gave me more pleasure than meat. They also gave my stomach more pleasure because I no longer felt sick all the time. I have not crossed the line over to the vegetarian world, but over the last few years, I have enthusiastically veered towards greens, grains, and beans. My stomach has felt better, my skin has improved, I never feel bloated, and I know I am doing something good for my body. Those wise elders were right, and I guess now I am one, so . . . eat your veggies.

some wisdom on vegetable cookery

1   Vegetables and salt are a match made in heaven. Don't be shy. When blanching vegetables use plenty of salt and use salt in the ice water for shocking, too. This helps keep the flavor and maintain a vibrant color.
2   Do not overcook your vegetables. Mushy vegetables are gross.
3   Don't be afraid to experiment with cooking vegetables in several different manners. Raw, roasted, braised, grilled, sautéed, drying. Each method will bring out a different, sometimes surprising flavor nuance.
4   Shop at your local farmers markets to get the best of the season at its peak. It really makes a difference. One of the most important aspects of cooking phenomenal vegetables is starting with the highest quality raw ingredients. So, particularly in this chapter, don't be afraid to substitute where it makes sense.
5   The recipes in this chapter are some of my favorite combos, but also feel free to keep it simple. Lemon juice, sea salt, and some olive oil can bring out the best in a vegetable.
6   The addition of cheese makes most vegetables better. A little Pecorino or Parmigiano-Reggiano goes a long way in adding the creamy, salty unctuousness that can make vegetables craveable.

curry roasted squash

serves 4

2	acorn squash, halved and seeded
8	garlic cloves, smashed
2 tablespoons	butter (¼ stick)
2 tablespoons	olive oil
1 tablespoon	kosher salt
1½ teaspoons	curry powder
1 teaspoon	chili flakes
8	sprigs thyme

1 Preheat the oven to 375°F.
2 Arrange the squash in a baking dish skin side down. Pour ½ cup water in the bottom of the baking dish.
3 Place 2 garlic cloves in the well of each half, followed by the butter, divided evenly.
4 Drizzle olive oil into the well of each squash, making sure to also rub some on the tops.
5 Season evenly with the salt, spices, and thyme.
6 Place in the oven and cook until the flesh is fork tender and golden brown, about 45 minutes. Remove from the oven and arrange all of the halves on a large platter for serving.

spring onion and whole wheat couscous tabbouleh

serves 4–6

3 cups	water
1 tablespoon	kosher salt
2 cups	whole wheat couscous
1	bunch Italian flat-leaf parsley, leaves only, chopped
	zest of 1 lemon
	juice of 3 lemons
3	baby spring onions, bulbs and tops, sliced thinly into rings
¼ cup	olive oil

1 Bring water to a boil and add the salt.
2 Put the couscous in a shallow, heat-safe container or bowl and pour the salted, boiling water over it. Cover with plastic wrap and let the couscous sit for approximately 5 minutes, so that the steam and water are absorbed.
3 Remove the plastic wrap and fluff the couscous with a fork.
4 Once the couscous has cooled, add the parsley, lemon zest and juice, spring onions, and olive oil. Mix well. Taste and add more salt if necessary.

grilled summer beans, garlic, mint, basil, parsley

serves 4–6

¾ cup	olive oil
5	garlic cloves, finely chopped
1 teaspoon	chili flakes
	zest and juice of 1 lemon
½ cup	roughly chopped Italian flat-leaf parsley
2 pounds	Romano beans
1 tablespoon	kosher salt
2	sprigs basil, leaves only
3	sprigs mint, leaves only

1   Light a grill to high heat.
2   While the grill is warming up, heat ¼ cup oil and the garlic together in a small saucepan over low heat. Cook until the garlic is lightly sautéed, no color and just aromatic.
3   Remove the pan from the heat, and set aside to let cool.
4   Once the garlic oil is cool, add the chili flakes, lemon zest, and parsley. Top with another ¼ cup olive oil. Stir to mix.
5   Put the Romano beans in a large bowl with the remaining ¼ cup oil and salt. Toss well, until the beans are coated.
6   Once the grill is very hot, place the beans on it and cook until well charred, slightly tender, yet still crunchy, 3–4 minutes.
7   Remove the beans from the grill and transfer to a large bowl along with the seasoned oil.
8   Add the lemon juice. Stir to evenly distribute the dressing over the beans.
9   Transfer the dressed beans to a serving bowl and garnish with the basil and mint leaves.

cucumbers, goat yogurt, shallots, mint

serves 4–6

3 large seedless cucumbers
2 shallots, sliced thin
zest of 2 lemons
1½ cups plain goat's milk (or other) yogurt, drained in a fine sieve
for 1 hour
juice of 1 lemon
¾ tablespoon kosher salt
2 tablespoons olive oil
3 sprigs mint, leaves only, torn
cracked black pepper
coarse sea salt

1 Halve the cucumbers lengthwise, and then slice each half into ¼-inch-thick half-moon pieces.
2 Place the sliced cucumbers in a large bowl along with the shallots and half the lemon zest.
3 Gently fold in the yogurt.
4 Add the lemon juice and mix to combine.
5 Season with salt just before you are ready to eat. (If you season with salt too early it will draw out too much water from the cucumbers and water down the dish.) Mix to combine.
6 Once seasoned, transfer to a large serving bowl and drizzle the olive oil over the top.
7 Garnish with the mint leaves, remaining lemon zest, black pepper, and sea salt.

cucumbers, goat yogurt, shallots, mint
pg 43

corn, leeks, mascarpone, buffalo butter
pg 46

corn, leeks, mascarpone, buffalo butter

serves 8–12

4 tablespoons	olive oil
3	leeks, white parts only, cut into ¼-inch half-moons (reserve the tender green tops of 1 leek to julienne very fine for garnish)
2	garlic cloves, sliced thin
3 tablespoons	buffalo milk butter
12	ears corn, shucked and kernels removed from cob
1 cup	mascarpone
1 tablespoon	kosher salt
10	small basil leaves

1 Heat a large sauté pan over medium low heat. Add the olive oil and leeks and sweat until tender, about 5–7 minutes. Add the sliced garlic and sweat for another 45 seconds.
2 Add the butter and once it has melted, add the corn. Cook the corn in the leek and butter mixture until warmed through and slightly tender, but with bite, 3–5 minutes.
3 Turn the heat down very low and gently fold in the mascarpone until it is evenly incorporated. (Be careful. If the heat is too high it will break.)
4 Season with the salt, mix to incorporate, and taste. Adjust if necessary.
5 Transfer to a large serving bowl and garnish with the basil and finely julienned leek greens.

cherry tomatoes, lemon, black pepper, oregano

serves 4–6

2 pints	cherry tomatoes, halved
1 tablespoon	sea salt
2 tablespoons	olive oil
	zest of 1 lemon, cut into fine, 1-inch julienne
15	twists black pepper
3	sprigs oregano, leaves only

1 Place the cut tomatoes on a serving platter cut side up.
2 Season with salt, olive oil, lemon zest, and black pepper.
3 Sprinkle with oregano leaves.

fennel, chili flakes, black pepper, balsamic, parmigiano

serves 4–6

4	bulbs fennel, trimmed and each cut into 6 wedges
4 tablespoons	olive oil
2 tablespoons	kosher salt
½ tablespoon	chili flakes
1 tablespoon	fennel seeds
	peel of 1 orange, 1 tablespoon zested, remaining cut into large pieces
3	whole sprigs rosemary, plus 1 sprig, leaves only for garnish
¼ cup	grated Parmigiano-Reggiano
15	twists of black pepper from a mill
2 tablespoons	aged balsamic vinegar
¼ cup	shaved Parmigiano-Reggiano
½ tablespoon	fennel pollen

1   Preheat the oven to 425°F.
2   Place the fennel in a large bowl and toss with the olive oil, salt, chili flakes, and fennel seeds. Transfer to a large baking dish, arranging each piece of fennel to lay flat on its side.
3   Scatter the slices of orange peel and rosemary sprigs on top and place in the oven. Roast until the fennel begins to caramelize and tenderize, 15 minutes.
4   Remove the dish from the oven to remove the orange and rosemary and add the grated Parmigiano-Reggiano. Place back in the oven to cook until the cheese starts to brown, another 10–15 minutes. The fennel should be tender but not too soft.
5   Remove from the oven and transfer to a large serving dish. Grind the black pepper over the top and drizzle with the balsamic vinegar.
6   Sprinkle with the shaved Parmigiano, orange zest, rosemary leaves, and fennel pollen.

cherry tomatoes, lemon, black pepper, oregano
pg 46

fennel, chile flake, black pepper, balsamic, parmigiano
pg 47

roasted pumpkin, parmigiano-reggiano, pine nuts
pg 52

roasted pumpkin, parmigiano-reggiano, pine nuts

serves 4–6

1	large (3–4 pound) pumpkin or winter squash, cut into wedges
2 tablespoons	kosher salt
	cracked black pepper
2 tablespoons	olive oil
2 tablespoons	butter (¼ stick)
2	sprigs rosemary, leaves only
¼ cup	toasted and roughly chopped pine nuts
¼ cup	Parmigiano-Reggiano, finely grated

1 Preheat the oven to 400°F.
2 Line the wedges of pumpkin in a baking dish. Position so that they stand upright, skin side down, and season evenly with the salt, pepper, and olive oil.
3 Dab the butter in little bits over the flesh of the pumpkin.
4 Sprinkle the rosemary leaves over the top.
5 Place in the oven, uncovered. Cook until the pumpkin is tender and caramelized around the edges, approximately 45 minutes.
6 Remove from the oven and transfer the pumpkin wedges to a serving dish. Top with the pine nuts and Parmigiano before serving.

tuscan kale stew

serves 4–6

1	bunch Tuscan kale
2 tablespoons	olive oil
2	garlic cloves, thinly sliced
½ tablespoon	chili flakes
2 cups	juice from a can of San Marzano tomatoes or tomato *passato*
1	15-ounce can cannellini beans, drained and rinsed
1 teaspoon	salt
½ cup	grated Parmigiano-Reggiano

1 Remove the leaves from the woody stems of the kale and wash leaves. Discard stems.
2 Heat a shallow saucepan over medium-low heat. Add the olive oil and garlic to the pan and sweat until aromatic but not browned. Add the chili flakes.
3 Rip the leaves of kale into rough, 4-inch pieces and add to the pan. Lightly sweat until well coated in the oil, about 3–4 minutes.
4 Add the San Marzano juice and cook the kale until tender, about 10–12 minutes. If using *passato* and it is a little too thick, add a cup of water, which will evaporate as it cooks. The kale will also release a bit of water.
5 Add the cannellini beans to the kale just to heat them through.
6 Season with the salt, stir to incorporate, and taste. Add more salt if necessary.
7 Transfer the stewed kale to a large serving bowl and top with Parmigiano-Reggiano.

whole roasted summer squash

serves 4–6

2 cups + 1 tablespoon	kosher salt
1	large (roughly 1 pound) globe-shaped summer squash or 4–6 smaller zucchini
4 tablespoons	olive oil
½ tablespoon	chili flakes, plus a pinch for garnish
1 tablespoon	fennel seeds
2	heads garlic, split
10	sprigs thyme
10	sprigs marjoram, 1 sprig reserved, leaves only for garnish
	juice of 1 lemon
1 tablespoon	coarse sea salt
3 tablespoons	breadcrumbs
2 tablespoons	grated Pecorino Romano

1 Preheat the oven to 350°F.
2 Spread the 2 cups salt in the bottom of a large, heavy-bottomed, Dutch oven.
3 Cut shallow slits on the skin of the squash or zucchini. This will allow the aromatics to penetrate.
4 Place the squash on the salt and drizzle 2 tablespoons olive oil over it.
5 Season with the remaining 1 tablespoon salt, and the chili flakes and fennel seeds.
6 Place the garlic around the squash and scatter the herbs over the top and around.
7 Cover the pot with either a lid or tented foil and place in the oven to cook until tender, approximately 45 minutes to 1 hour. (This is the rare instance where you want your vegetables to get slightly soft.)
8 Once cooked, remove the squash from the pot and transfer to a tray or platter that will catch the juices that spill out. While it is still hot, use a knife to split the squash open into quarters, using your fingers to pry it open.
9 Transfer the split squash to a low bowl for serving. Surround with some of the juices.
10 Dress with the lemon juice and remaining olive oil. Season with the coarse sea salt and pinch of chili flakes.
11 Sprinkle the breadcrumbs, Pecorino, and reserved marjoram leaves over the top before serving.

asparagus, harissa yogurt

for the harissa

1 pound	Fresno chiles
1 cup	olive oil
3 tablespoons	coriander seeds
3 tablespoons	cumin seeds
3 tablespoons	caraway seeds
8	garlic cloves, finely chopped
1 tablespoon	sweet paprika
1 tablespoon	smoked paprika
1 tablespoon	hot paprika
½ cup	tomato paste

1   Preheat the oven to 475°F.
2   Toss the Fresno chiles in 2 tablespoons olive oil and spread evenly on a sheet tray. Place in the oven and roast until tender and skin is blistered, approximately 12 minutes.
3   Transfer the peppers to a bowl and cover with plastic wrap. This will allow the peppers to steam and help the skin to come off more easily. Once cooled, use your fingers to remove the skin from each before cutting in half lengthwise. Use the edge of your paring knife to gently scrape away the seeds.
4   Lightly toast the coriander seeds in a dry, small sauté pan over medium-low heat. Constantly shake the pan so the spices move around a little and don't burn. Toast until aromatic. Transfer to a small bowl.
5   Repeat this process two more times for the cumin and caraway seeds.
6   Combine the toasted seeds in a spice grinder and coarsely grind. Set aside.
7   Blend the peppers in a food processor until pureed.
8   Cover the garlic in a small saucepot with ¼ cup of the olive oil. Heat on low and sweat just until aromatic, 2–3 minutes.
9   Transfer the garlic and its cooking oil to a mixing bowl. Add the pureed peppers, ground spices, paprikas, and tomato paste. Mix to combine.
10   Transfer to a container that can be tightly sealed, like a mason jar or Tupperware. Cover with the remaining olive oil, seal, and place in the refrigerator where it can stay for at least a week or two.

for the asparagus and finish

2	bunches asparagus
1 cup	Greek yogurt
1½ tablespoons	harissa
	kosher salt, for the water

1   Break off the woody bottoms from the ends of the asparagus. If you are feeling fancy, peel the asparagus halfway up each stalk. Set aside.
2   Mix the yogurt and harissa together in a bowl.
3   In a large saucepan, heat 1 inch of water and season it with enough salt that it tastes like the ocean. Add the asparagus and cover, steaming for approximately 1–3 minutes. Asparagus should be tender but still bright green and crisp.
4   Use tongs to remove from pan and arrange on a serving platter. Serve alongside the harissa yogurt sauce, using it as a dip. Feel free to eat with your fingers!

chickpeas, cauliflower, smoked paprika, preserved lemon

serves 4–6

¼ cup	olive oil, plus more for frying
1	head cauliflower, cut into 2-inch pieces
2	garlic cloves, thinly sliced
2 cups	juice from a can of San Marzano tomato juice or tomato *passato*
1 tablespoon	smoked paprika
1 teaspoon	hot paprika
¾ tablespoon	kosher salt
2 tablespoons	chopped preserved lemon
1	15-ounce can chickpeas, drained and rinsed

1   Heat a wide sauté pan over medium-high heat. Add 2 tablespoons olive oil and, in batches if necessary, sauté the cauliflower until it starts to become tender and caramelized. Repeat with any remaining cauliflower, adding a bit more olive oil if necessary. Remove from the pan and set aside.

2   Add the remaining 2 tablespoons olive oil to the pan along with the sliced garlic. Sweat until aromatic, about 1 minute, then add the tomato juice, smoked and hot paprika, salt, and 1 tablespoon preserved lemon. Cook for 8–10 minutes to let the flavors meld together.

3   Add the chickpeas to the sauce before transferring the cauliflower back to the pan. Mix so everything is incorporated. Taste and season with more salt if necessary. Garnish with the remaining 1 tablespoon preserved lemon before serving.

slow roasted tomatoes, coriander, fennel seeds

serves 4–6

12	medium heirloom variety tomatoes, halved
1 tablespoon	kosher salt
2 tablespoons	olive oil
1 tablespoon	fennel seeds
1 tablespoon	coriander seeds, cracked

1   Preheat the oven to 275°F.

2   Lay the halved tomatoes cut side up in one layer on a sheet pan or baking dish.

3   Season the tomatoes with salt, olive oil, and the spices.

4   Place the tomatoes in the oven and roast for 2 hours. They should shrink slightly, with crinkled edges, but retain some of their juices—not completely dried out, just concentrated.

carrots, white anchovies, feta

serves 4

4	medium carrots, sliced thinly on a bias with a mandoline
3 tablespoons	olive oil
	juice of 1 lemon
2 teaspoons	Aleppo pepper
1 teaspoon	kosher salt
12	marinated white anchovies
6 ounces	feta cheese, crumbled into ¼–½-inch chunks
¼ cup	Italian-flat leaf parsley, leaves only

1 Place the carrots in a large mixing bowl. Dress with 2 tablespoons olive oil, the lemon juice, and 1 teaspoon Aleppo pepper. Toss well to mix.
2 Season with salt, adding more if necessary.
3 Transfer the seasoned carrots to a platter or large serving bowl. Scatter the anchovies and feta.
4 Drizzle the remaining 1 tablespoon olive oil and dust the remaining Aleppo over the top.
5 Garnish with the parsley leaves.

slow roasted tomatoes, coriander, fennel seeds
pg 58

potatoes, fresh chillies, mint, feta
page 63

grilled avocado, pistachios, bottarga

serves 4–6

4	avocados
3 tablespoons	olive oil
¼ cup	celery leaves
	juice of 2 lemons
¼ lobe	bottarga
¼ cup	pistachios, coarsely chopped
	pinch chili flakes
1 teaspoon	coarse sea salt

1 Preheat a grill to high. If you don't have a grill, use a stovetop grill pan over high heat.
2 Split the avocados in half lengthwise, keeping the skin on. Remove the pit.
3 Drizzle a touch of the olive oil on the surface of the avocado meat. Place the avocado halves flesh side down on the grill. Grill until slightly warm and there are char marks on the avocado, about 1–2 minutes. Remove them from the grill and carefully peel the skin away.
4 Lay the avocados on a platter, grilled side up. Drizzle with the remaining olive oil and squeeze the lemon juice over the top. Using a vegetable peeler, shave bottarga slices over the dressed avocados and garnish with the celery leaves and pistachios. Finish with the chili flakes and coarse sea salt.

potatoes, green chilies, mint, feta

serves 4–6

6	medium Yukon Gold potatoes
	juice and zest of 2 lemons, peel of 1 cut into big pieces and
	peel of other finely grated for garnish
5	garlic cloves
5	sprigs thyme
2	sprigs rosemary
¼ cup + 2 tablespoons	olive oil
5	serrano chiles, 2 whole and 3 cut into very thin rings
2 tablespoons	kosher salt
1 tablespoon	coarse sea salt
3	sprigs mint, leaves only, torn
4 ounces	feta cheese

1   Preheat the oven to 350°F.
2   Place the potatoes in the center of a piece of foil large enough to wrap them completely. Add the large pieces of lemon peel, garlic, thyme, rosemary, 2 tablespoons olive oil, the 2 whole serrano chiles, and kosher salt. Use your hands to toss and coat the potatoes. Wrap the foil into a tight package. Wrap again with another large piece of foil to ensure steam stays inside.
3   Place the foil package on the center of a sheet pan and place in the oven. Cook until potatoes are fork tender, approximately 45 minutes to 1 hour.
4   Remove from the oven and open foil. Leave for a few minutes to cool slightly.
5   While still warm, use a knife to gently break the potatoes into rustic pieces and transfer to a platter.
6   Season with sea salt, lemon zest, lemon juice, and the remaining olive oil.
7   Garnish with torn mint leaves, large crumbles of feta, and the remaining sliced serrano chiles.

favas, peas, ramps, farro

2 cups	farro
	kosher salt
¼ cup + 2 tablespoons	olive oil
½ cup	ramp bulbs, sliced into 1/8-inch-thick pieces
½ cup	ramp tops, finely diced
2 cups	fava beans, blanched and cooled
2 cups	peas, blanched and cooled
1	bunch of Italian flat-leaf parsley, leaves picked and chopped
	juice of 2 lemons
	zest of 1 lemon
½ cup	Parmigiano-Reggiano, shaved
½ cup	Pecorino Romano, shaved

for the farro

1   Heat the oven to 300°F.
2   Spread the farro in an even layer on a sheet pan. Toast in the oven until just slightly golden with a nutty aroma, approximately 10 minutes.
3   Bring a large pot of water to a boil and generously season with salt. Add the farro and cook until tender but still with an al dente bite, approximately 12 minutes.
4   Drain the farro and spread evenly onto a sheet pan to cool.

for the ramps and finish

1   Place a wide sauté pan over low heat and add 2 tablespoons olive oil.
    Add the sliced ramp bulbs and tops and sweat until tender, about 5 minutes.
    Set aside to cool.
2   In a large mixing bowl, combine the cooled farro, remaining olive oil, ramp tops and bottoms, fava beans, peas, parsley, lemon juice, and zest.
3   Mix in ¼ cup of each cheese.
4   Taste, season with more salt if necessary, and mix gently to incorporate.
5   Transfer to a serving bowl and garnish with the remaining cheese.

tomato braised eggplant

serves 4–6

6	Japanese eggplants
6 tablespoons	olive oil, plus more for frying
	kosher salt
3	garlic cloves, thinly sliced
3 cups	Arrabbiata sauce (see page 112)
¼ pound	smoked ricotta salata (if you can't find smoked you can use regular, but the smoke adds a unique flavor)
1 teaspoon	chili flakes
¼ cup	breadcrumbs
1	bunch basil, leaves only

1 Cut each eggplant in half lengthwise, then halve the pieces again crosswise.

2 Heat a large sauté pan over medium-high heat and add ¼ cup olive oil. In batches, add the eggplant and sauté cut side down until golden brown, about 3–4 minutes. As eggplant is browned remove from the pan and set aside. Season with salt. Repeat with remaining eggplant until all is sautéed, continuing to add oil as needed.

3 Add another 2 tablespoons of olive oil to the pan and lower the heat. Add the garlic and sweat until aromatic, about 1 minute.

4 Add the Arrabbiata sauce. Transfer the browned eggplant back into pan and cook on low heat until cooked through and completely tender, about 8 minutes.

5 Transfer the eggplant to a platter and top with the heated sauce.

6 Garnish with ricotta salata, chili flakes, breadcrumbs, and basil.

198

Olive oil. Cheese. Pasta. Ice Cream. Pizza. These were my major food groups. It's not surprising that for years my weight had been slowly creeping up. I was always so busy or stressed or surrounded by enticing food that I was able to brush it aside for too long. I mean, delicious food was my job, right? There were lots of excuses and some mortifying experiences along the way (including one bottom-of-the-barrel moment when a fellow subway passenger presumed I was pregnant and offered to give me her seat) but it was the day that I stepped on the scale and 198 looked back at me that I knew I had to get my ass in gear. Holy shit. How could that be? At 5'6", 198 not only doesn't feel great, it's also just not healthy.

Genes were partially to blame. I've inherited the "Robbins stomach," as we like to call it, a tendency to hold extra weight in my stomach area, which I can't really help. But a big chunk of the weight gain was an uncontrolled diet and a workaholic lifestyle. I know it's not all that PC to talk about being "fat," but that's exactly how I felt each morning when I rolled out of bed and got dressed. In my restaurant life, I lived in my chef's coat and used it as a way to hide the weight—from myself and others. But a year out of restaurants meant a year in street clothes. I couldn't hide in the kitchen anymore.

It wasn't like I'd never tried to shed the extra pounds. I always believed I could lose weight through exercise alone, and technically I had been a gym goer for years because I would pay for a membership that I never really used. I joked that it was my monthly donation to the charity of Equinox. There were times I would cancel my membership and rely on personal trainers and boot camps for a while, but lots of dollars and time spent all added up to money not-so-well-spent because the weight never came off.

Just before I left A Voce, I joined a gym again. I was intent on getting in shape, though part of the motivation was the great roof deck. My new membership came with a free session of Pilates, which seemed like an activity demanding far more grace than I am capable of offering. Mainly because I didn't want to let the free session expire unused, I had a crack at it. I was clumsy and uncoordinated, but also intrigued. I signed up for ten sessions and haven't looked back. I began to feel real, very positive effects on my very broken restaurant body. Everyday life got easier. I became so much more flexible that bending down to tie my shoes was no longer an awkward stretch. I could feel more support in my core just walking down the street. I started going three times a week—not something I could really afford, but easy to justify because I wanted to get serious about my health. I knew that this time, if I spent the money I would go. I felt accountable to the investment of private Pilates classes on top of a gym membership, and also to my instructor, who I knew would be waiting for me. I looked forward to my visits to the Pilates machines which, although they struck me as strangely archaic and similar to what I imagine medieval torture chamber machines looked like, fixed my body, even though they kicked my ass.

Back to the scale. I had been doing Pilates religiously for months and 198 still stared me in the face. Even after all of this hard work, I was still almost a size 16 and my much stronger ab muscles were still covered up by more than thirty pounds of fat! The time had come. If I wanted to lose weight, I had to re-examine my diet.

First up: Reminding myself to eat breakfast and lunch everyday. This was hard. My routine was coffee in the morning, work until I hit the point of starvation around two or three in the afternoon, then gorge on whatever I felt like eating until I was full. Not healthy. At both restaurants I had to taste new dishes constantly. It was supposed to be a bite or two, but if I liked it, I would just continue to "taste" until it was gone. Also, as a chef who particularly enjoys carbonara, baked ziti, and steak, portion control and food discipline were kind of foreign concepts. Not only is food my livelihood, it's my passion, so my social life revolves around food, too. I was always the one at a group dinner sneaking the last bite from a communal plate. A pint of ice cream or a whole pizza in one sitting was not all that unusual. I had always managed to avoid partying and other vices that can become pitfalls for chefs. But I realized that food was my vice. What a terrible irony! When I had tried to diet in the past, it was mostly through plans to cut out carbs and sugar. Those sometimes worked, but only for short periods of time—it was kind of a ridiculous prospect, given that my calling is Italian food. I cook pasta. That's what I do. How long could I really cut it out completely from my diet?

Enter a very good friend and chef Todd Stein, who told me he lost fifteen pounds in four weeks on Weight Watchers. *Yeah, yeah*, I thought. *Good for you, but that's SO not for me.* Isn't it turkey and broccoli all of the time? How could I survive on such a diet, let alone be a happy, functional chef? But here I was, two-thirds of the way into what was supposed to be my year for getting healthy and I was still overweight. I wasn't breathing right. My ankles hurt all of the time. Honestly, I was willing to try anything. I promised myself and my girlfriend that the day after my forty-third birthday, on February 22, I was going to start. I made sure to include a stipulation that if it didn't work after two weeks, I was out. I lost five pounds in the first week.

The transition included a few speed bumps. Weight Watchers is all about portion control and choices. On the first day, after twelve years of cooking Italian food, when I saw that one tablespoon of olive oil is three points, I lost my shit. Just to give you some perspective: I got twenty-six points a day. Breakfast, lunch, dinner, snacks, drinks—everything I ingested or imbibed in a twenty-four-hour period had to add up to that. So three points for olive oil seemed ridiculous. Nevertheless, I wanted to give this thing a real shot, so for the first time in my life, I measured and I put that three points' worth of olive oil in the pan and tried to sauté garlic and immediately realized that normally, I would have used five times that amount. This sucked already. Then I checked the points for the pasta that would go with my sauce and saw that I could reasonably have two ounces. That was easily half of my typical portion. How could this be right? I was going to starve. I didn't want to cave one meal in, so begrudgingly, I went with it. In hindsight, what could have been one of the worst meals I've ever eaten became one of the most life-changing. It forced me to recalibrate my brain. Pasta with broccoli became broccoli with pasta. I used greater portions of ingredients like tomato paste and anchovies instead of more olive oil. A slice of pizza is now accompanied by a salad instead of seven other slices. Don't get me wrong, it's not that easy. There are sacrifices that are harder to make. I eat a third of a croissant, not a whole one. Bagels are only on very, very special occasions. Beloved burgers at The Spotted Pig are halved and shared. Manhattans are almost never ordered. Steak is only three ounces per meal. Ice cream is no longer devoured from the container, but instead out of an espresso cup. If someone had told me five years ago that I would measure my gelato and olive oil before eating it, I would have thought they were insane. But here I am.

My love affair with Pilates continues. I remain clumsy and uncoordinated; I still go left when my trainer says right. But I'm also thirty-five pounds lighter and my joints are functional again. I can buy the clothes I want. I don't feel sick after I eat. Pilates and mindful eating are a priority for me, and though I'm back in a restaurant, I won't let go of them because they're how I maintain balance and well-being. Most people think my career is my biggest accomplishment. But I know that getting healthy and losing the extra weight during my year off is my greatest achievement yet. Before I left A Voce, I don't think I would have ever said doing something for myself was more important than something work-related. I would have always put the restaurant first. And I think I had gotten so used to feeling crappy that I didn't know what it was like to feel healthy and balanced. Now that I've had a taste of what that feels like, there's no going back. It's my favorite addiction. One that I won't be kicking anytime soon. Not even for a Michelin star.

all salads are not created equal

Salads are a great, quick, healthy meal (for the most part). They don't require a lot of prep time. They don't require a lot of cooking. They can be very filling. And it kind of makes you feel good to say you ate salad for lunch, and even better to say you ate it for dinner. Like anything, the key to creating exceptional salads is starting with quality ingredients. Though this is a rule to live by for all of your cooking, it is perhaps never more important than with salads. The raw or lightly cooked nature of most salads makes it really hard to hide behind anything. It is essential to buy the best vegetables, the best vinegars, cheeses, and olive oil, etc. Skimp a little on your soup—but never on your salads. And please, please, do not buy shitty mesclun mixes; if you do, you'll never embrace a true love of greens and all of the varieties out there.

Building a beautiful salad is also about achieving the perfect balance of flavors and textures. There are many opportunities to break out of the basics. Breadcrumbs and nuts for crunch. Playing with citrus juices and vinegars for acid. Cheeses for creamy saltiness. Salads don't need to be built around lettuce. In my eyes, they are really anything consisting of some kind of vegetable and some kind of dressing.

house "italian" dressing

makes 1 cup

This is the most versatile dressing. It doesn't matter what you put it on, somehow it always works: romaine, zucchini, artichokes, potatoes, beets—let your imagination run wild. When I first came up with this dressing, I made it by hand in a mortar and pestle. I basically just assessed what I had in the house, threw in a bunch of ingredients that I love, and smashed away. I surprised myself with the wonderful result; it tasted like a better version of the Wishbone Italian that I grew up with. It's now become a staple both at home and at work—so I guess you can call it my "house" dressing.

1	head garlic, cloves peeled and finely chopped
2	shallots, peeled and finely diced
¾ cup	olive oil
3	sprigs oregano, leaves only, roughly chopped
3	sprigs parsley, leaves only, roughly chopped
1 teaspoon	chili flakes
¼ cup	red wine vinegar

1   Place the garlic and shallots in a small saucepan and cover with the olive oil. Place over low heat and slowly cook until they are soft and aromatic with no color, about 8–10 minutes. Remove from the heat and allow to cool.
2   Once cool, add the chopped herbs and chili flakes.
3   Just before you are ready to use the dressing, whisk in the vinegar. (Waiting prevents the acid from discoloring the herbs.)

70

my semi-healthy caesar   serves 4–6

Me and Caesar salad go way back. Not only is it one of my favorite things in the world to eat, but I also have a lot of warm and fuzzy Caesar salad memories. It was the dish I made when I threw my first dinner party for friends at age fourteen, using my grandmother's wooden Caeser-salad bowl. And it was the first thing I learned to make in my very first restaurant job. (And then had to make daily five-gallon buckets of it!) Unfortunately, it is loaded with cheese, egg yolks, and olive oil, ingredients that were not welcome on my newfound path to healthy eating. Let's face it, we all pretend we are eating healthy if we are eating a salad, but traditional Caesar dressings (and lots of other creamy dressings) can be a big, fat calorie offender. Still, it was important for me to find an alternative to one of my go-to comfort foods, so I discovered that using yogurt instead of oil and eggs still allowed me to keep the garlicky, anchovy flavors of this wonderful dressing without ruining my diet.

5	garlic cloves
5	anchovy fillets
3 tablespoons	Dijon mustard
1 tablespoon	black peppercorns
¼ cup	red wine vinegar
5	dashes Tabasco
1 tablespoon	Worcestershire sauce
	juice of 1 lemon
1 cup	plain yogurt
½ cup	grated Parmigiano-Reggiano, plus ¼ cup for finishing
3	hearts of romaine, outer leaves discarded, cored to separate and wash leaves
	cracked black pepper

1   Place the garlic, anchovies, mustard, black peppercorn, red wine vinegar, Tabasco, Worcestershire, and lemon juice in a blender. Blend on medium-high speed until a paste is formed and the garlic and peppercorns are completely crushed and blended. Transfer to a mixing bowl.
2   Gently fold in the yogurt and ½ cup Parmigiano-Reggiano. I like my dressing thick, but you can thin it out a touch by adding a drop or two of water.
3   Place the clean, dry romaine leaves in a large mixing bowl. Add ½ cup dressing and use your hands to gently mix until all the leaves are coated. (Store the rest of the dressing in a tightly sealed container in the fridge and keep on hand for the week.)
4   Top with the remaining grated Parmigiano and a few twists of black pepper.

house "italian" dressing
pg 70

apples, gruyère, little gem
pg 74

apples, gruyère, little gem   serves 4–6

There is something magical about the combo of tart crunchy apples and the nutty pungency of Gruyère cheese. The most common association people have with Gruyère is its role as the best part of French onion soup, melted and oozing over the top—but here, it's used raw and grated. The other unexpected thing about this salad is its departure from my Italian "roots." But it's nice to get out of my flavor comfort zone once in a while.

4	granny smith apples, sliced into ⅛-inch-thick wedges
3 heads	Little Gem lettuce, broken into individual leaves
1	lemon
3 tablespoons	olive oil
	kosher salt
	black pepper
4 ounces	gruyère cheese

1 Place the apples and lettuce leaves into a mixing bowl.
2 Halve the lemon and squeeze its juice directly into the bowl. Add the olive oil and salt to taste, tossing to coat evenly.
3 Transfer to a platter and grind black pepper over the top.
4 On the large side of a box grater, grate the gruyère cheese over the top so it showers the whole salad.

watercress, grapefruit, crispy chickpeas   serves 4–6

This has the two elements that I think make a perfect salad: peppery greens and tart-but-sweet fruit. I'm a fan of watercress for both the flavor and the texture; the stems give great crunch to any salad. I add crispy chickpeas for a little protein and also to serve as another crunchy note. You can make your own chickpeas by baking them in the oven for about an hour, but they are also readily available at many grocery stores. Feta is a staple in my fridge and balances out the spice of the greens.

2 bunches	watercress
3	ruby red grapefruits, peeled and segmented
3 tablespoons	olive oil
2 tablespoons	red wine vinegar
	kosher salt
4 ounces	feta cheese, crumbled into large chunks
½ cup	crispy chickpeas

1 Place the watercress and grapefruit in a mixing bowl. Add both the oil and vinegar and toss gently to dress. Season with salt, to taste.
2 Transfer to a serving platter and top with the feta and crunchy chickpeas.

chicory, bacon, red wine vinaigrette   serves 4–6

I first had this salad in a little trattoria in Modena, Italy. After eating at the famed Osteria Francescana, Massimo Bottura's three-star Michelin restaurant, I asked him for recommendations of where to eat simply and locally–nothing fancy. This salad was the perfect start to a meal of cured meats and pastas. As probably noted, I don't use a ton of pork in my recipes, but I do include it in this one, as the giant fatty chunks of rendered, smoky bacon make the dish. In this case, chicory refers to any number of possible bitter greens, from radicchio to frisée to escarole. Choose your favorite or mix and match.

½ pound	slab bacon, cut into ½-inch cubes
2 heads	frisée, core cut off and leaves broken
2 heads	treviso radicchio (the long variety), chopped
2 tablespoons	olive oil
¼ cup	red wine vinegar
	freshly ground black pepper

1   Place the bacon in a sauté pan on medium-low heat and render slowly until the fat melts and the pieces are tender, but slightly crisp on the outside. Remove from the heat and set aside, keeping the bacon bits in the rendered fat.
2   Place the frisée and radicchio in a large mixing bowl and mix with the reserved bacon and the rendered fat, olive oil, red wine vinegar, and black pepper to taste.

nectarines, goat cheese, arugula, balsamic   serves 4–6

This salad hits all the notes that excite the palate: sweet, acidic, bitter, spicy, creamy, tangy. It's an ideal way to showcase summer produce and is quick and easy, but still looks elegant and sophisticated. You will notice I don't dress the arugula in this salad; I prefer to leave it crisp and gently kissed by the dressed ingredients in this dish.

6	nectarines, halved, pitted, and cut into ½-inch-thick slices
	sea salt
	freshly ground black pepper
3 tablespoons	olive oil
2 tablespoons	high-quality balsamic vinegar
4 ounces	goat cheese, broken into ½-inch chunks
1½ cups	arugula

1   Arrange the sliced nectarines on a serving platter. Season with sea salt and black pepper, then drizzle with the olive oil and balsamic.
2   Garnish with goat cheese.
3   Arrange arugula over the top.

celery, orange, almonds
pg 78

celery, orange, almonds

Celery is a completely underrated vegetable in my opinion. It's got so much going for it: texture, unique flavor, and a subtle salinity. While it usually lies quietly in the background, in this dish, the celery is an equal to the citrus, balancing the sweetness and acid the orange provides. The almonds add an earthy component. This is a quick preparation that I like to make for lunch, or even as a side dish to accompany winter fish recipes. It's a bright salad sure to counter the winter blues.

1	head celery, trimmed, celery leaf reserved
6	oranges, segmented, reserving ¼ cup juice
½ cup	raw almonds, roughly chopped
4 tablespoons	olive oil
	sea salt
	freshly ground black pepper

1. Using a vegetable peeler, peel the tougher outer stalks of the celery. (You will not need to peel the inner pieces or "the heart.") Slice on the bias into crescents about ⅛-inch thick.
2. Place the celery in a bowl and add the orange segments. Use your hands to gently combine and transfer to a large plate or platter.
3. Drizzle with the olive oil, then the reserved orange juice.
4. Season with sea salt and pepper.
5. Garnish with the chopped almonds and reserved celery leaf.

escarole, lemon, herbs, breadcrumbs   serves 4–6

I've always loved escarole for its crunch and distinctive bitter flavor. The inner leaves tend to be a bit milder than the outer. Some people get scared by bitter; but if balanced with other ingredients, especially acid, it is just right. I love to mix fresh herbs into salads to add flavor, depth, and pop. Soft herbs like parsley, basil, and chives work great here.

2	heads escarole, outermost leaves removed
¼ cup	basil leaves
¼ cup	parsley leaves
1	small bunch chives, cut into 1-inch lengths
2	lemons
3 tablespoons	olive oil
	kosher salt
	freshly ground black pepper
¼ cup	toasted breadcrumbs

1   Cut the core off the escarole. Tear the leaves by hand into large pieces and place into a bowl.
2   Mix with the basil, parsley, and chives.
3   Halve each lemon and squeeze the juice over the greens. Drizzle with the olive oil and season with salt and pepper. Gently toss to combine.
4   Transfer to a serving bowl and top with the breadcrumbs.

travel essentials

I was destined to love travel. It's in my blood. My maternal grandparents owned a resort in Wisconsin called Brown's Lake. It was one of those *Dirty Dancing* type places, similar to resorts in the Catskills where people would come retreat for weeks at a time during the summer, eat lavish meals, lounge by the pool, canoe in the lake, and dance the night away. It's where my mother spent her summers growing up and eventually, when she married my father, where they spent their weekends away from Chicago when they were first married. Later on, they brought me and my brother.

I was quite young when they sold our only family heirloom, but I still remember small, peculiar details, like how my aunt used to leave large packs of Trident gum alongside little notepads for me in the room. Though Brown's Lake has been out of the family for decades, I've held on to those strange tiny memories, and the legends and stories live on, frequently recalled at family meals. The lake setting, the history, the hard work, and especially tales of the food are memories that continue to bring the family together. I can only imagine the different life I might have had if they had held on to it. Would I have continued to spend my summers there instead of going away to Jewish camp? Who knows? Maybe I would have been running it by now!

Another major influencer on my penchant for travel is my dad's love for it. I'm not sure where his adoration originated; perhaps it started with Brown's Lake, or just grew out of a general curiosity about the world, fueled by an attraction to a bit of temporary luxury. Either way, we traveled a lot as a family. We often went to Los Angeles to visit my great-grandmother and great-aunt. The highlight was definitely the mid-century motel we always stayed in—an old-school-feeling lodge with rooms that surrounded a pool. I recall breakfasts of fresh-squeezed orange juice and snack-pack sized boxes of Corn Flakes. Similar to the Trident gum, it's a strange detail to hold on to, but as a chef, attention to detail is everything, so I guess I started young.

Our family travels took us to Israel, London, Paris, and Italy, as well as around the states, from Maine to Vegas. We stayed at the elegant Connaught Hotel in London when I was twelve; no twelve-year-old should be allowed to travel like that. My sophomore year in college, we celebrated my mother's sixtieth birthday at an intimate inn in Maine. We ended a national parks tour at an upscale spa in Sedona, Arizona. I knew I was privileged, and maybe even a little bit spoiled, but I was raised to never take any of it for granted. My father did not grow up wealthy. He put himself through both college and medical school and worked his ass off to provide the very best for our family: the best education, the best home and seemingly, the best travel. If my father wasn't closely studying opera librettos or watching Georgetown basketball on a Saturday afternoon, he had the Relais & Châteaux book in hand, planning the next adventure. That book was usually reserved for my parents' solo trips, which always included the finest in Michelin star dining and unbelievable hotels and castles. Even when my brother and I weren't on the trip, I would still benefit from hearing all the details of the setting, the linens, the service. When we went for day-long jaunts into New York City from suburban Connecticut, my mother would always know exactly what hotel in what neighborhood had the best bathroom to use. I guess it's no mystery that I, too, came to love and appreciate food, travel, and fancy hotels. Like many wander-lust college kids, I traveled after graduation, and while I shared many of the hallmarks of my peers doing the same, specifically a backpack and multicity Eurail pass, the similarities pretty much stopped there. I definitely didn't embrace the crowded, dingy hostels and I wasn't going to eat my way through Europe by grabbing any quick bite I could get. Even as a twenty-two-year-old on a budget, I was seeking out cute inns and the best meals my wallet could manage.

Perhaps it's not surprising then that when I left A Voce for my very extended vacation, I knew some form of travel would be part of the equation. I wasn't sure what that meant, exactly: how long, where to go, and when to go. But I knew a rare opportunity for carefree time spent away from hectic NYC was an essential part of my break from restaurants. Once fall was closing in, the time seemed right for a big trip. So, ever my father's daughter, instead of planning one, I decided to plan two. Extravagant, I know. It had been two years since my last trip to Italy and I was craving that Italian inspiration, so the first trip would be three weeks exploring the north of Italy, centered around a grand finale truffle hunt in Piemonte. I would return Stateside for Thanksgiving and then the biggie: my first trip to Asia for the whole month of December. I put the wheels in motion and started the planning.

It was an overwhelming task to plan two such momentous trips but I didn't really have anything else going on, so planning basically became my day job. Maybe because I already knew Italy so well, I found solace in my comfort zone, and dove straight into the details of the first trip, focusing all of my energy on organizing the *ultimate* trip. I had been there many times, studied every region, knew so many cities and towns. But this time, since I was after the perfect trip, the perfect hotels, the perfect meals, the perfect neighborhoods, the perfect itinerary, I became obsessed. While putting together a plan for Italy was easy, organizing what to do and where to go in Asia left me feeling somewhat paralyzed. It was a lifelong dream of mine to go there, and I had never had this much time, or rather made the time, to make it happen. Now that I was faced with actually planning this once-in-a-lifetime trip, I felt crushed by the weight of all the build-up. It was unfamiliar territory and I had no idea where to start. As with most things in my life, if I wasn't good at it, I procrastinated. But now there was no more delaying. I finally had the chance to get lost in a completely foreign world, literally and figuratively, so the question was, where to go? I decided on Hong Kong, Vietnam, and Thailand. Narrowed down slightly from an entire continent, but still so much to figure out: what cities, what beaches, how to get everywhere?

Where usually I'd be putting my mind towards meticulously planning a menu or a new dish in a restaurant, constantly striving for some form of perfection in my profession, now I found myself channeling that energy into these trips. I was three or so months into my extended vacation and clearly seeking something on which to focus. I even convinced myself that I might have found my second calling as a travel consultant! I researched like a maniac. I scrutinized guidebooks, travel websites, hip hotel guides, and apps. I always think that getting intimately acquainted with my destination before landing is the key to trying to live like a local no matter where I am. That said, while I love getting the logistics of travel right, I also look forward to the unforeseen moments of spontaneous pleasure and discovery that punctuate a trip. A stroll into a no-name cafe in Modena to have the best cappuccino of my life. A five-mile trek through the streets of Milan to get to a highly anticipated restaurant only to find that the random buffalo milk cheese store along the way was way more memorable than the actual destination. Disappointment with overly fancy and underwhelming hotel food in Ko Lanta, Thailand, that sent me, frustrated and hungry, wandering down the beach until I stumbled upon some of the most delicious food I ate in a month in Asia.

In the end, both trips ended up being spectacular in their own right. Filled with ups and downs, as in life, travel is never perfect. There are detours, disappointing hotels. But the most important thing was immersing myself outside my world for two months. Not to focus on what was next, but just to exist in a different world. Being in strange places, taking myself out of my comfort zone and constantly churning thoughts about my career.

On New Year's Eve, I arrived home from Asia to a pizza at the door, courtesy of my neighbors. It was the best welcome home to New York. I knew it wouldn't be long before my travel high wore off and I had to face the reality that it was about to be a new year, and I was still without a job or itinerary to let me know where I would end up. There was no more time for leisurely sight-seeing, it was time to make a plan.

aperitivo hour

There are many, many things I love about Italy and its culture, but I'm not sure there is anything I embrace more than the ritual of aperitivo hour. There is a certain end-of-day serenity, or beginning-of-evening anticipation, enjoyed while sipping a negroni or Aperol spritz in an open piazza, people watching and munching on chips, olives, and nuts. It is a moment to wind down and ready your palate for a late evening dinner with assorted delicacies that vary depending on where you are. For example, in Venice, you can just hop from *cicchetti bar* to *cicchetti bar*, enjoying different small bites along the way that often include marinated vegetables, enticing crostini, sardines, and anchovies. Adopting the foods, cocktails, and feelings of the aperitivo hour is a fantastic way to kick off a dinner party at home, or even keep your guests full and happy with a whole evening of grazing.

the perfect negroni

Every time I drink a negroni it brings me back right back to Italy. Not sure what I like more: the drink itself, or the feeling of sitting and watching the early evening go by. Negronis are a perfect balance of bitter, sweet, and aromatic flavors. While you can use other sweet vermouths, Carpano Antica is my favorite. It's a rich, full-bodied spirit with a serious history to it (it was created in 1786)! There are so many amazing gins on the market now with varying profiles. Pick one that suits your tastes.

1 ounce Gin
1 ounce Carpano Antica Vermouth
1 ounce Campari
1 4-inch piece orange peel (no pith)

Fill a rocks glass with ice. Pour the Campari, then vermouth, then gin over the ice. Stir until well mixed. Garnish with the orange twist.

aperol spritz

An Aperol spritz is a fantastic drink to both start off and finish the night because they are (somewhat) low in alcohol and quite refreshing. I have many fond memories of being in Venice, starting the afternoon off with a spritz and a *panino* as a snack, while milling about outside the fish market with the locals.

2 ounces Aperol
2½ ounces prosecco
1 ounce club soda
1 piece 4-inch piece orange peel (no pith)
olive on a skewer (optional)

Fill a large wine glass with ice. Pour the Aperol, prosecco, and soda over the ice. Mix well, garnish with an orange twist, and if you want to really feel like a Venetian, add an olive on a skewer.

vermouth on the rocks

There is no real recipe needed for this; I just wanted you to know how lovely a drink this is. It is low in alcohol and so flavorful and simple. When you want to start your evening really light, this is the way to go.

vermouth
ice
1 piece 4-inch piece orange peel (no pith)

Pour vermouth over ice in a rocks glass, finish with orange twist.

bees knees

This is a classic American cocktail that combines my favorite spirit with two of my favorite ingredients and goes down a little too easy. It is traditionally served up, but as with all my cocktails, I prefer it on the rocks.

for the honey syrup

1 cup water
1 cup honey

Combine the honey and water in a small saucepan over low heat, cooking until the honey dissolves. Remove from the heat and transfer to a glass container. Reserve.

for the cocktail

2 ounces gin
¾ ounce lemon juice
½ ounce honey syrup

Put the gin, lemon, and honey syrup in a cocktail shaker with ice and shake well. Pour into a coupe or, as I prefer, serve in a rocks glass over ice.

grappa and grapefruit perrier

Grapefruit Perrier is like Fresca without the sweetness and such a welcome staple into my life. I developed my love of grappa around the same time as I discovered it, which is perhaps why they seemed like they might combine to make a great cocktail. I was right.

1 ounce grappa
¾ ounce honey syrup (above)
½ ounce grapefruit juice
½ ounce lemon juice
5 ounces grapefruit Perrier
1 piece 4-inch piece grapefruit peel (no pith)

1   Mix grappa, honey syrup, and both juices in a cocktail shaker over ice.
2   Fill a tall Collins type glass with ice and pour over.

Top off with the Perrier. Garnish with a grapefruit twist.

vermouth on the rocks
pg 84

bees knees
pg 85

orange and spice marinated olives

makes 1 quart

I know that this is not exactly reinventing the wheel, but the flavor combination takes these mild olives to a whole new level. In my opinion, Castelvetrano olives are the best varietal of olives around for eating on their own. They aren't too strong but have just enough flavor and texture to whet the palate for other snacks and accompany your first cocktail of the evening.

1 quart	Castelvetrano olives
	zest and juice of 1 orange
1½ tablespoons	coriander seeds, cracked
1½ tablespoons	fennel seeds, coarsely ground
½ tablespoon	chili flakes
2	sprigs rosemary
½ cup	olive oil
5	garlic cloves, smashed

1   Combine all the ingredients in a bowl, stirring well to mix and set aside to let the flavors mix together for at least 1 hour. If you can, prepare these a day or two before so that they sit and marinate together; they'll be even better.
2   Remove the rosemary before serving.

spiced pumpkin seeds

makes 2 cups

These spiced seeds always remind me of the fall and hollowing out pumpkins and squash. Even though the flesh is usually most prized, I always keep the seeds to roast, salt, and eat. If you don't have pumpkins or squash on hand, you can buy ready-to-go pumpkin seeds and roast them before tossing them in the spice mix.

2 cups	pumpkin seeds
2 tablespoons	olive oil
1 teaspoon	kosher salt, plus more to taste
1 teaspoon	sweet paprika
1 teaspoon	smoked paprika
½ teaspoon	ground cumin
1 teaspoon	Aleppo pepper

1   Preheat the oven to 325°F.
2   Toss the seeds in a bowl with the olive oil and salt and spread them in an even layer on a sheet pan. Toast in the oven for 5–10 minutes until slightly golden and aromatic.
3   Combine the spices in a mixing bowl. Transfer the seeds to the bowl of spices and toss well to coat. Taste and add more salt if needed.

chili spiced popcorn

serves 4

When I started to be more mindful of how I ate, this became a staple snack because it is flavorful, low in fat, and filling. You can certainly use microwave popcorn but there is just something satisfying about doing it the old-school way.

3 tablespoons	olive or canola oil
½ cup	popping corn
1½ tablespoons	sweet paprika
1½ tablespoons	hot paprika
2 teaspoons	garlic powder
½ tablespoon	ground chili flakes
1½ teaspoons	fine sea salt

1   Place a heavy-bottomed pot over low-medium heat. Add the oil and then the corn kernels. Cover and cook while occasionally shaking the pan until all (or most of) the corn is popped. You will hear the pops dwindling and silence when it is done.
2   While the corn is popping, combine all the spices in a small bowl.
3   Transfer the popcorn to a large mixing bowl and toss in the spices until coated.

sea salted potato chips

serves 4

Nothing compares to homemade, right-out-of-the-fryer potato chips. The most important thing to getting a crisp, light chip is extracting as much of the potato starch as possible before frying, and you do this by soaking and rinsing the sliced potatoes. Do not skip this step. I prefer my potato chips to be so thin that you can almost see through the raw potato slices.

4	Yukon Gold potatoes, peeled
3 quarts	canola oil
	fine sea salt

1   Use a mandoline to slice the potatoes into even, very thin slices that are almost see through. Place them in a large bowl and cover with cold water. Let them soak in the refrigerator overnight.
2   Transfer the potato slices to a colander and place it under cold running water for 10–15 minutes to rid them of any excess starch that remains.
3   Arrange the wet potato slices in single layers between paper towels to dry them as much as possible.
4   Place the oil in a large heavy-bottomed pot with sides high enough that you are not at risk of the oil bubbling over. Heat the oil to 325°F.
5   In small batches, gently fry the chips until just crispy and slightly golden, but not brown.
6   Use a spider or slotted spoon to remove the chips from the hot oil and transfer to paper towels to drain excess oil. Salt them immediately. Continue this process until all of the chips are fried and salted.

chili spiced popcorn
pg 89

traditional bagna cauda
pg 93

onion dip

Admit it—you love Lipton French Onion Dip as much as I do! It might be my guiltiest pleasure and one of the only processed foods I eat, so one day I set out to make my own. It definitely doesn't fit into the healthy category, and probably isn't any better for you than the processed version, but I feel just a little less bad about myself as I indulge because I made it from scratch. This is certainly not as quick and easy as dumping dehydrated French onion mix into sour cream, but the results after cooking your own onions for 1–2 hours are really worth it.

1	head garlic
2 tablespoons	olive oil
2 tablespoons	butter
7	large onions, thinly sliced
½ cup	water
1½ cups	sour cream
1½ cups	crème fraîche
1 teaspoon	garlic powder
1 teaspoon	onion powder
25	grinds of black pepper
⅓ cup	finely chopped chives
1 teaspoon	kosher salt, plus more to taste

1   Preheat the oven to 350°F. Place the head of garlic on its side and trim ¼-inch off the top, exposing the top of the cloves. Drizzle with a bit of olive oil and completely enclose it in aluminum foil. Place it in the oven for about 45 minutes, depending on the size. Once the garlic is completely softened and caramelized, remove it from the oven and set aside to cool, then squeeze the cloves from the papery skin and finely chop. Set aside.

2   Heat a wide, heavy-bottomed pan or pot to low. Surface area is key because if the onions are overcrowded, it will take a lot longer to caramelize them. Add the olive oil, and the butter. Once the butter melts, add the onions and stir to coat them in the fat.

3   Add the water and cover the onions with a piece of parchment paper cut to a size that just fits inside the circumference of the pan or pot.

4   Cook for about 2 hours on low heat until the onions are deeply caramelized and dark golden brown. You might need to add small amounts of water along the way to prevent scorching, so keep an eye on it.

5   Once browned, remove the onions from the pan and cool. Chop them very finely or buzz them in a food processor.

6   Mix the sour cream and crème fraîche together in a bowl.

7   Add the garlic powder, onion powder, and black pepper. Gently fold in the caramelized onions and roasted garlic.

8   Fold in the chives, season with salt, taste, and adjust by adding more salt if necessary. Serve with raw vegetables or Sea Salted Potato Chips (pg 89)

traditional bagna cauda

makes 1 quart

I have made many versions of *bagna cauda* in my restaurants, but didn't truly understand the dish until I had the pleasure of devouring it in its homeland, Piemonte. In the tiny town center of Asti sits a modest trattoria which serves this surprising gem. A large platter of too many vegetables to remember—beets, fennel, peppers, cardoons—ranging from raw to roasted, was delivered to my table along with a candle-lit vessel, the distinct purpose of which is to keep the prized anchovy sauce warm. (In English, *bagna cauda* means "warm bath.") The vegetables and sauce would have been enough for me on my own, but it was topped off when the chef offered to cook an egg in the anchovy sauce that remained after the vegetables were gone. And as if the dish and evening weren't perfect enough, he went and shaved truffles in it!

2 cups	anchovies in oil, drained
3 cups	milk
2½–3 cups	olive oil (just enough to cover mixture)
1	head garlic, cloves peeled and finely minced
¼ cup	red wine vinegar
	assorted raw and roasted seasonal vegetables
	grilled rustic bread

1   Soak the anchovies in the milk for 1 hour. This will relieve the fish of some of its salt. Drain the anchovies from the milk and rinse them in cold water. Use towels to pat them dry.
2   Chop the anchovies either very finely by hand, or by pulsing in a food processor. (If you are up for it, it is better to do this by hand so they don't get too mushy.)
3   Put ¼ cup olive oil into a small pot and place over low heat. Add the minced garlic and sweat until aromatic, with no color, 2–3 minutes.
4   Add the chopped anchovies and cover with enough olive oil to cover the mixture. Cook on very, very low heat for 1½–2 hours. The anchovies will break down further and their flavor will meld with the garlic to create a thick sauce/dip. Stir occasionally so nothing sticks to the bottom. If you have a riser to put over the burner, it's a good idea.
5   Remove the pan from the heat and stir in the red wine vinegar. Transfer the anchovy sauce to a serving bowl or leave in the pot to keep warm. Serve alongside the vegetables and grilled country bread.

salted anchovies, salsa verde, bread, butter
pg 96

cured anchovies, pink peppercorns, orange
pg 96

salted anchovies, salsa verde, bread, butter

serves 2–4

Perhaps my biggest *aha* moment in Italy was the discovery of anchovies doused in an eggy salsa verde. This is not a combination that had ever crossed my mind before and when put atop a chunk of hearty bread swathed with creamy butter, the flavor experience was transformative in its simplicity. It has everything you want in a little snack; or, if you're like me, you would happily let this serve as your meal.

1	baguette
¼ pound	really good butter
½ cup	Salsa Verde (pg 200)
2 ounce	can anchovies in oil, drained

1 Rip the bread, spread the butter, dip in the salsa verde, add an anchovy, eat, and repeat!

cured anchovies, pink peppercorns, orange

serves 4

Cured white anchovies are a good starter anchovy if you haven't yet fully embraced the little fish. They are fresh anchovies that are deboned and marinated in olive oil and vinegar and are milder than their salt-cured counterparts, but still acidic and flavorful in their own way. I think they are best used as an accompaniment to a vegetable, as with the carrots on page 57, or paired with mozzarella, or as in this dish, just simply enhanced with citrus and spice. This combo is inspired by one of my favorite treats found in Venetian *cicchetti* bars.

20	pieces boquerones (white anchovies)
1 tablespoon	pink peppercorns, cracked
	zest and juice of half an orange
2 tablespoons	olive oil

1 Lay the anchovies skin side up on a plate and sprinkle with the cracked peppercorns and orange zest.
2 Drizzle all over with the orange juice and finish with the olive oil.

oysters, condiments, beer

serves 4–6

For many years, I had a fairly lukewarm stance on oysters. But, while on a trip to Napa, I made a lovely afternoon stop at the Hog Island Oyster Co. in Tomales Bay in Marshall, California, right where the oysters are harvested. It was basically self-service: we did the shucking, drank the beer, and chose our own condiments. It was just about as simple and fresh as it gets. Location is everything, so the idyllic setting probably helped, but my fondness for the briny delicacy grew in that very moment. At home, I take my cues from that experience and just throw the oysters on ice, put out a few oyster knives, and let the festivities begin. The recipe for the mignonette is fairly traditional—but classics are classic for a reason!

for the mignonette

3	shallots, finely minced
⅓ cup	red wine vinegar
	cracked black pepper

Combine all the ingredients in a small mixing bowl. Stir to blend.

for the oysters

2 dozen	oysters
	mignonette
3 tablespoons	fresh horseradish, grated
2	lemons, cut into wedges
	hot sauce (tough to beat good old Tabasco for oysters)

Serve the fresh oysters alongside the mignonette and other condiments. (Don't forget the beer!)

deviled egg toast

I always pass on deviled eggs because I don't like the boiled egg white, and although I'm a sucker for the filling, it's not generally acceptable to dive into it leaving the rest of the egg behind. I came up with a solution that celebrates my favorite part of a deviled egg. I typically finish each crostini with *bottarga*, which is pressed, salted, and dried mullet or tuna roe, but truffles would be equally delicious. (I've also been known to eat this spread on toast with hot sauce for breakfast.) Salty, spicy, tangy all in one crunchy bite. Such a step up from a boiled egg white!

for the garlic aioli

1	head roasted garlic (see how to roast garlic in the Onion Dip recipe on page 92)
3	garlic cloves
3	egg yolks
	juice of 2 lemons
1 cup	canola oil
	zest of 1 lemon
½ teaspoon	kosher salt, plus more to taste

1   Place the roasted garlic, raw garlic, egg yolks, and lemon juice in a blender. Blend on high to break down the ingredients and mix them together.
2   With the motor still running on low speed, slowly drizzle the oil into the garlic and lemon mixture until all has been incorporated and you have a thick mayonnaise consistency.
3   Transfer the aioli to a mixing bowl and fold in the lemon zest.
4   Season with the salt, taste, and add more if necessary.

for the deviled egg spread

2½ dozen	eggs
1 cup	garlic aioli (recipe above)
⅓ cup	Dijon mustard
¾ cup	crème fraîche
½ teaspoon	kosher salt, plus more to taste

1   Place the eggs in a large pot and cover with cold water. Bring to a boil over medium-high heat. Once the water comes to a boil, turn off the heat and cover. Let the eggs sit for 11 minutes.
2   Drain the water and immediately transfer the eggs to a large bowl of cold water with ice in it. This "shocking" method will stop the egg from cooking. Once the eggs are completely cool, remove from the cold water and, with the shell still on, break each egg in half in order to remove just the yolk. Discard the shell and, if you'd like to, save the whites for salads or snacking.
3   Place the yolks in a food processor. Pulse the processor until the yolks are broken up.
4   Add the garlic aioli and mustard and pulse until well combined.
5   Transfer the mixture to a bowl and gently fold in the crème fraiche.
6   Season with the salt, gently stirring to combine. Taste and add more salt if necessary.

for the crostini

24	pieces country bread (like ciabatta or baguette), sliced on the bias into pieces approximately 1-inch thick
¼ cup	olive oil
	deviled egg spread (previous page)
½ teaspoon	ground chili flakes
1	lobe bottarga, peeled

1   Preheat the oven to 375°F.
2   Brush each piece of bread with olive oil. Arrange the bread in an even layer on a sheet pan and place it in the oven to get crusty and golden on the outside, but still soft in the middle. This should take approximately 3–5 minutes.
3   Transfer the deviled egg spread to a plastic storage bag and seal, or a pastry bag if you have one. If using a plastic storage bag, snip a small hole in the corner that is about a ¾-inch long.
4   Pipe the spread onto the surface of the toasted bread, sprinkling each with ground chili flakes. Using a microplane, grate the bottarga over the top of each slice before serving.

crostini, nduja, ricotta, fig   makes 6 pieces

Nduja is a spicy, spreadable sausage typical to the southern Italian region of Calabria. While it has become more popular in recent years, it can still be somewhat difficult to find, but the search is worth it.

3 tablespoons	olive oil
6	slices of crusty country or rustic bread (baguette, ciabatta, etc.), sliced on the bias approximately 1-inch thick
½ cup	nduja sausage, room temperature
¼ cup	ricotta
6	fresh figs (or dried if not in season), halved
18	small basil leaves
	sea salt

1   Drizzle 2 tablespoons of the olive oil on the bread slices. Preheat the oven to 400°F and toast the bread until golden, but still with a little chewiness. (Also works great on a grill.)
2   Spread the nduja on the toast and top each with a dollop of the ricotta.
3   Garnish with the figs and basil.
4   Lightly season with sea salt and drizzle with the remaining olive oil.

crostini, nduja, ricotta, fig
pg 95

sungold tomatoes, garlic, fettunta
pg 104

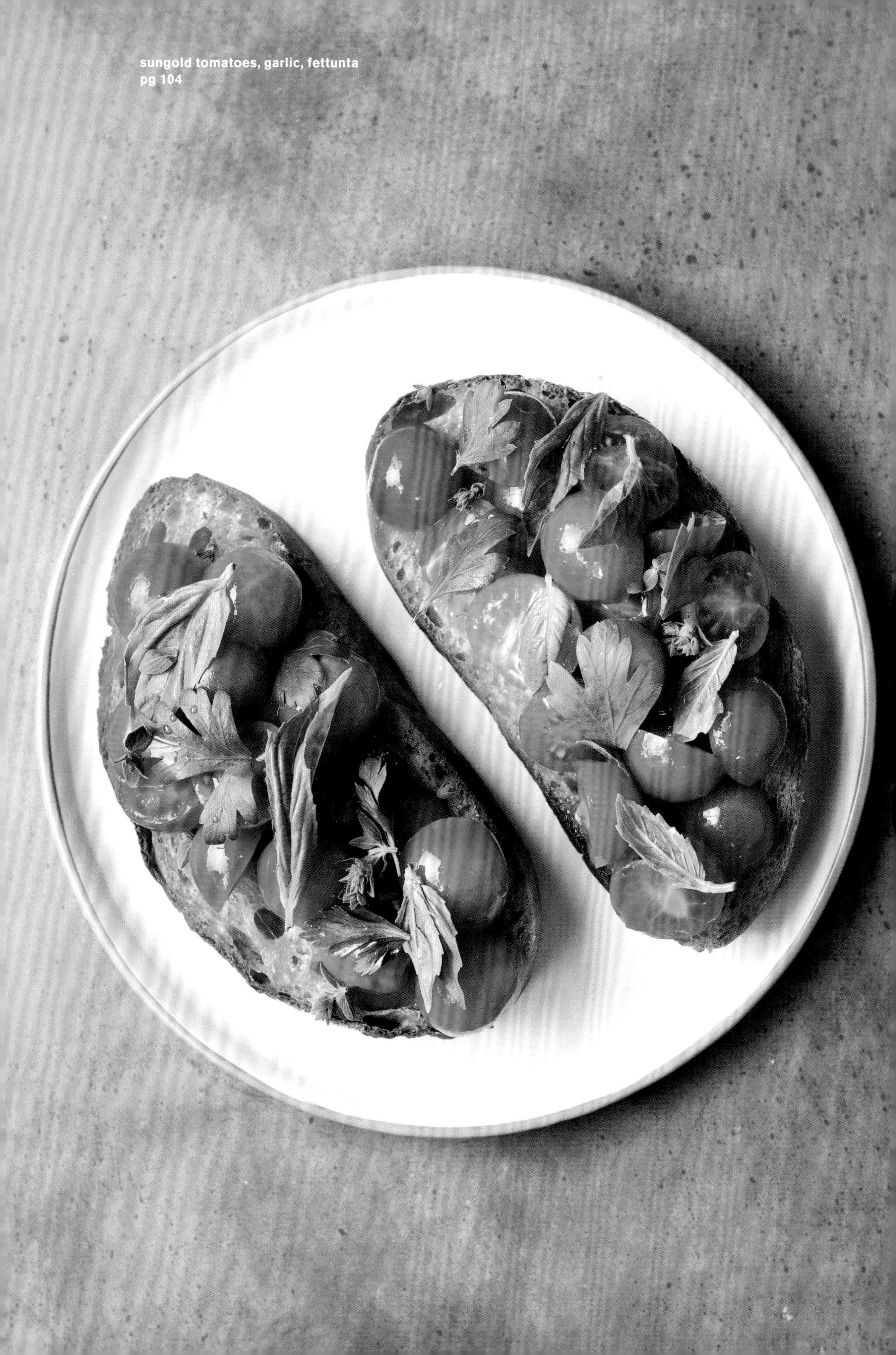

sungold tomatoes, garlic, fettunta

makes 6–8 pieces

This is a fancier take on traditional tomato bruschetta in part because of the *fettunta*, which is just toasted bread drizzled with olive oil and rubbed with garlic.

2 pints	Sungold tomatoes
5 tablespoons	olive oil
1½ teaspoons	sea salt
¼ teaspoon	chili flakes
1 teaspoon	fennel pollen
6–8	slices of crusty, country bread
2	garlic cloves, peeled
2 tablespoons	minced chives
	parsley leaves

1   Slice the tomatoes in half, lengthwise. Add 3 tablespoons of the olive oil and season with the sea salt, chili flakes, and fennel pollen. Gently stir to combine and let sit for 10 minutes, until the natural juices emerge from the tomatoes.
2   Preheat the oven to 400°F, or if you prefer, heat your grill.
3   Drizzle the remaining 2 tablespoons of olive oil on the bread and toast or grill until golden.
4   Remove from the heat and rub the garlic cloves on the bread.
5   Spoon the marinated tomatoes on the toasted slices of bread, along with a little bit of the juice.
6   Garnish each with the minced chives and 3–4 parsley leaves.
7   Serve immediately. (The bread will get soggy quickly.)

warm mussels, tomato, garlic bread

makes 6 pieces

I first had this dish in a little *cicchetti* bar in Venice. It was a humble joint run by a proud husband and wife team equipped with only a hot plate and a microwave that still managed to turn out really special food. I initially just stopped by for my evening spritz, but was pleasantly surprised when I also found this unique take on a *crostini* using the best of Venetian seafood.

1 pound	mussels
5 tablespoons	olive oil, plus more for finishing
2	garlic cloves, sliced
½ cup	dry white wine
1 cup	Arrabbiata sauce (page 112)
6	slices rustic bread, cut 1-inch thick
1 teaspoon	chili flakes

1   Thoroughly clean the mussels in cold water and remove their beards.
2   Heat a pot over medium heat and add 3 tablespoons olive oil.
3   Once the olive oil is warm, add the garlic and sweat for 10–15 seconds.
4   Add the mussels and white wine.

5   Cover and cook (in batches if necessary) for 3–5 minutes, periodically checking to
    see if the mussels are opening. Remove from pan as they open and set aside.

6   When all the mussels are cooked and cool enough to touch, remove the meat from
    the shells and set aside, submerged in the cooking liquid. (There is a lot of flavor
    goodness in there.)

7   Preheat the oven to 400°F or heat your grill. Drizzle and rub the remaining
    2 tablespoons olive oil on the bread and toast until golden and slightly crunchy.

8   While the bread is toasting heat the Arrabbiata in a small saucepan. Add the
    mussels along with 2 tablespoons of the mussel cooking liquid. Warm through.

9   Top the crusty bread with the mussels and sauce. Drizzle with olive oil and season
    with chili flakes.

baked salami, brown bread, mustard   makes 6–8 pieces

This dish features in my top five favorite family food memories. My parents used to
have gigantic Super Bowl parties, and this was my mother's specialty dish. I could see
how the ingredient combo might seem a little weird and maybe even gross, but it was
a hit every year, and I assure you it will be devoured by your party guests. This recipe
calls for two salamis, because one is never enough. Of important note: standard, Aunt
Jemima-type syrup is preferable because, for some reason, it just works better! I've tried
to use fancy, real maple syrup and it's just never the same. This is one family recipe that
needs no changing or fancifying; it's perfect just as it is.

2	kosher salami (Hebrew National if you can get them)
1½ cups	syrup
1	loaf rye or brown bread, sliced
½ cup	Gulden's spicy brown mustard

1   Make three diagonal slits on two sides of each of the salami. Place the salami in a
    small baking dish and cover with the syrup. Marinate in the fridge overnight, making
    sure you turn the salami a few times.

2   Preheat the oven to 350°F.

3   Drain the excess syrup so that you are left with enough in the bottom that it comes
    about ¾-inch up the sides of the salami. Cover the baking dish with foil and place it
    in the oven. Bake for 25 minutes and then flip over the salami, so they brown evenly.
    Cook for another 15 minutes and then remove the foil. Put the dish back in the oven
    for another 10–15 minutes, or until the salami is golden brown and slightly crispy.

4   Use tongs to turn and coat the salami in the syrup before transferring it to a cutting
    board.

5   Cut each salami into 14 slices. Be careful, the sugars from the syrup are very hot.

6   Serve directly on the cutting board with the sliced bread and a pot of Gulden's
    mustard.

from red sauce to truffles

A few years back, when trying to nail down a menu for a high-profile celebrity's seaside lunch in the Hamptons, a couple of my chefs and I debated what would be best for the al fresco meal in the warm weather. One of them suggested pasta and I blurted out, "I mean I'm Italian and even I don't like to eat pasta in the summer!" They both looked at me, completely confused, and said, "You do know you're not Italian, right?"

Italian food and culture have been so central to my life and work that it is now part of my makeup. So the answer to that question in that moment should have been, *No, clearly I do not know that I am not Italian.*

Come on—maybe just a little?

In fact, I am not even a little Italian. I am of Eastern European descent and grew up very culturally Jewish. But it's where I grew up that gave me my first taste of the Italian way of eating that I have come to love. New Haven, Connecticut, is a community rich in Italian-American culture and, most importantly, food. While many of my childhood food memories involve brisket, chicken soup, and other Jewish delicacies, still more of them involve baked ziti, pizza, calzone, and fettuccine alfredo. "Red sauce" was what I knew of Italian food. I knew *ricott* and *muzz* from the Italian groceries my mother would take me to shop weekly. I had olive oil, but I never really understand how special it could be. I didn't know what Northern Italy was; I didn't know what Southern Italy was. I didn't know that Italy had twenty different regions and, with them, essentially twenty different cuisines.

My first trip to Italy was with my parents during my freshman year of college. I was a nineteen-year-old shithead and I didn't appreciate where I was, which in my idiotic mind didn't really matter because I didn't particularly want to be there anyway. I remember certain foods and certain towns, and I remember eating rabbit for the first time after it was cooked over an open fire in a Tuscan hilltop town. I remember the dark, windy road to get there. I remember eating a lot of asparagus. But even with these pretty romantic sounding, outstanding food memories, that trip was not my 'aha' Italian moment. I'm not really sure there ever was just one moment or a particular bite that made me believe that Italian was the way to go. I think it was several experiences piled up—a gradual growth that saw me always pulled back to my early Italian inspirations. I loved the trips as a young girl in Connecticut to the Italian markets with my mother, and I loved the Italian inspired dishes I came across or created in all the kitchens I worked in coming up in this industry. Even at the beginning when I was mostly cooking "New American" food with lots of different influences, I found myself constantly returning to the Italian ingredients that resonated with me the most. Olive oils, cheeses, vinegars, pastas. The basics, but the basics that are created with such craftsmanship and history that they struck a chord in me. Always. This is maybe why if I could pick one thing to do all day in the kitchen it would be to make pasta. I lose myself in the repetition and the drive to make each piece perfect. It's mind blowing how three simple ingredients can be so transporting. Even before I settled into Italian kitchens, I always found a way to be the person who makes the pasta, and in this way I was able to continuously study the craft and the differences in dough, and serve my fascination.

But, still, it took me nine years of cooking professionally before I decided to fully take the plunge into Italian culture and food and I didn't know then that I would never come up for air. I was coming up on two years into my very first sous chef job and I was ready to move on. I worked long hours, six days a week in a punishingly hot and tense kitchen under a stressed-out chef. It's not that I was miserable, because I wasn't. I was twenty-eight years old and felt it was time for a change. A big change. And I also feared that if I didn't travel abroad then, I would never do it. I had no obligations in life, other than my job. So I decided to up and move to Italy—no visa, no Italian language, no understanding of Italian geography and regional identities. It was scary and exhilarating all at the same time. (Now it all sounds very similar to my decision to leave A Voce fifteen years later. I guess I am a creature of habit, and that it's true what they say: history does repeat itself.)

It was my first true introduction to the real work of handcrafted pasta and regional Italian cuisine. From the *pastaia* with an ashy cigarette hanging out of her mouth, to the seasoned mama in the kitchen, to the tightly coiffed chef-owner, everywhere I went I saw the real repetition and art of making beautiful, tender, fresh pasta. Everyone had their own method, but the common denominator was heart and soul (and of course flour, eggs, and water). Some didn't use machines, so everything was hand rolled with a giant rolling pin every day and it wasn't easy. It took strength and dexterity, but was also surprisingly communal. The chef would have her friends come by in the afternoon and they would all make the pasta together. Still others preferred to do it all on their own and it would be done with the production team before I even woke up. No matter who was making it or how they liked to do it, I found pasta-making mesmerizing.

My first trip was at nineteen, but my most recent trip was in the fall of 2013, in the midst of my hiatus from work. While I was dying to spend time in the south, it only seemed logical to spend this time in the north, because I wanted the last stop to be in Piemonte during the highly revered white truffle season. I have been eating and cooking and loving truffles for years, but until then, had never gone straight to the source. Figuring I would never again get this much time off from work in November, I would be a fool not to take advantage of the timing. I spent a solid two months planning and plotting this trip, particularly looking forward to the finale: a truffle hunt in the hills of Alba, Piemonte.

The trip started with some of my favorite places to eat and drink in Milan, a city that is often overlooked by tourists, but that has become close to my heart over the years. A stop in Venice was a pure study in *aperitivi* and *cicchetti* bar culture. Bologna, while it used to be one of my favorites and is often considered the food capital of Italy, seemed sort of drab this time. But that was quickly counteracted by a jaunt to an out-of-the-way inn and farm, Antica Corte Pallavicina, in the countryside of Emilia Romagna outside the city of Parma. We have this one area to thank for amazing cured meats such as *culatello*, the heart of the prosciutto, balsamic vinegar, and Parmigiano Reggiano—making this stop one of pure inspiration. Driving up the long, treacherous road to get to the inn was thrilling—in an I'm excited but also scared shitless kind of way. The first thing I was greeted with upon arrival was an intense barnyard smell before being escorted to a rustic, but still elegant, room above the salon and restaurant. It took a day to discover that the barnyard smell was emerging from the aging room where the *culatello* hangs for months, waiting for its debut. Sort of gross, but also inspiring. Meals at the inn were filled with *negroni* cocktails, freshly produced *salumi*, whole roasted guinea hens, rich gnocchi with truffles, tastings of different aged *culatello* and, to top it all off, a *grappa* tasting. When you don't have anywhere to be and your room is a mere twenty-five feet away from the dining room, *grappa* tastings are in order. It was where I had my first tryst, and now full-blown love affair, with the strong Italian spirit. It was the first time I ever really understood that *grappa* has flavor other than that of gasoline. I was able to recognize the nuances that make it so special. The inn arranged for a tour of a Parmigiano factory where the smell of sweet milk and aging cheese still lingers in my mind. An out-of-the-way *trattoria* brought a grandma cooking tiny ravioli, or *occhi* (eyes) as they were called, filled with the famed

Parmigiano. Simple, but different than anything I'd ever had before, and scrumptious. In fact, everything seemed new to me in this region, despite my having spent time in Emilia Romagna on my sabbatical fifteen years earlier. It was as though I was looking with fresh eyes and tasting with a virgin palate.

Next stop was Modena. Aah, Modena. One of my favorite towns anywhere, not just because it is where I reached the pinnacle of properly made cappuccino euphoria. The town itself is beautiful, elegant, quiet, and small. The main purpose in going to Modena was to eat at Osteria Francescana, the three-star Michelin restaurant run by chef Massimo Battura. It had been high on my list for a long time and so I came to the meal with a lot of anticipation, but the four-hour lunch of elevated delicacies did not disappoint. The highlight, aside from the famous five stages of Parmigiano dish, was really having Massimo Bottura spend time at the table, in particular the moment when he fed me *culatello* by hand! As we sat, he and his lovely wife, Lara, shared so much about the Modena they clearly adore and have so much pride in. Where to eat, what markets to poke around, and a suggestion for what turned out to be the best sandwich I think I've ever eaten. Inside the covered food hall in Modena, nestled amongst the mounds of cheese, piles of vegetables, rows of meats and fish, is a little sandwich shop. I generally don't even like sandwiches, but the combination of fatty *cotechino* sausage, salsa verde, aioli, and balsamic on crusty baguette was a bite like no other I have ever encountered. Fatty, rich, acidic, textured, and an amalgamation of regional ingredients—it was nothing short of brilliant. Thank you, Massimo! For the *culatello*, but also letting me in on that sandwich secret.

At this point I was not sure that anything could top cheese production, three-star chefs, balsamic producer tours, and the amazing Antica Corte Pallavicina. How could truffles in Alba possibly top these experiences? Truffles were saved for the last part of the trip, but I worried that I built up this truffle thing too much. Was it going to be a let-down?

The first stop in Alba was a truffle store. Walking into the store smelled like the captivating first moment of opening a box of truffles that I was used to getting delivered to restaurant kitchens back home. But instead of a momentary whiff, the smell stayed with me; it permeated the entire space. There were fresh truffles, most likely hunted that morning, truffle salts, truffle pastes, and truffles shavers. Here's the thing: I CRIED. The truffles brought actual tears to my eyes in the best possible way. It was the strangest visceral reaction I have ever had to anything. I was overcome with emotion over a truffle, a dirty little tuber from the ground! It was so bizarre. I tried to hide it but my travel companion laughed and noted that I had tears running down my face. Was I really that excited about the earthy, sweet, inimitable smell of a truffle? I guess it was written on the tears streaming down my face. The seven-course truffle lunch that followed was obviously amazing, but as is usually the case, there is nothing like a simple preparation to show off the special qualities of an ingredient. And so, for me, nothing really compares to a bowl of buttered pasta with heaping shavings of the earthy tuber on top, which became a daily Piemontese ritual for me. When in Rome (or Alba in this case)!

Several days were spent traveling throughout Piemonte, in Alba, and surrounding towns, tasting other regional delicacies like *bagna cauda* and rich *fonduta*, and wine tasting at prestigious wineries like GAJA. But, all was building toward the culmination of the trip, which was meant to be a truffle hunt in the hills of Alba. As I mentioned before, the entire itinerary had been planned around this one sole morning. The plan was to meet these Italian men and their dog, who is trained to seek out the truffle by smell. Clearly, the gods were against me because Piemontese skies brought three days of rain. And truffles are not hunted in the rain. Who knew? We showed up to the meeting place and the lady looked at us like we had seven heads. There was no truffle hunting that day. I couldn't believe it. I was on the verge of truffle tears again, but this time very disappointed, depressed truffle tears. That lasted about three minutes until I realized that I was still in Alba, and that I could spend the rest of the day indulging in a very long, rainy-day, red-wine-and-truffle-fueled lunch.

A secret sandwich. A truffle at the source. A trip to a local market or a fancy schmancy Michelin star meal. A standout olive oil. Homemade pasta. A great *ricott*. In many ways, Italy has fed my soul and penetrated my mind. I'm not sure when it first took hold, was it childhood days in New Haven? My first trip at nineteen? It is of no matter, what is most interesting is that during my year off, Italy inspired me in new ways that I will never forget. And I returned even more certain—I must be Italian.

pasta

I have spent many years studying and perfecting my pasta cookery, which, when done correctly, is both an art and a science. If you follow these guidelines, you will be on the road to cooking pasta like a pro.

1   Use a bigger pot than you think you need. There should be enough space for the pasta to move around so that it cooks evenly.
2   Heavily salted water is essential for great pasta. Just as you want your sauce seasoned properly, the pasta should be well-seasoned too. The key is to cook it in very salty water.
3   Never, ever put oil in your pasta water. It prevents the sauce from sticking to the pasta.
4   Don't drain your pasta into a colander in the sink. You'll lose all the cooking water—an important ingredient in pasta-making. Some pots have a basket insert, which is a larger version of the pasta baskets we use in restaurants; if your pot doesn't have one, you can purchase one separately. Alternately, you can remove pasta from the pot with tongs (for long shapes) or a spider (for small ones).
5   Pasta cooking water is your friend! As pasta cooks, some of its natural starches leach out into the water. These starches add body and salinity to your sauce. Stir in a little pasta water during the final stage of cooking, when you combine the pasta with the sauce.
6   Fresh pasta is not necessarily better than dried pasta. They are just different. And buying expensive artisan pasta isn't essential to making a delicious dish. I happen to love De Cecco brand. It cooks evenly, has good flavor, and consistent quality.
7   Disregard the cook times on packaged pasta; they are usually overestimated, and don't take into account the additional time the pasta cooks once it's in the sauce. I usually cook store-bought dry pasta for 1 or 2 minutes less than suggested. You'll get a feel for the appropriate timing once you've mastered finishing your pasta in sauce.
8   You need 1½–2 cups of sauce per pound of pasta. A pound of pasta usually serves 4.
9   Remember that pasta water, properly salted, will also add salt to your sauce. Keep that in mind and be careful when making and seasoning sauces. If a sauce becomes too thick or salty, you can always thin a sauce out and adjust the salt by adding small amounts of water.
10 "The Marriage" in pasta is crucial. Those last few minutes that the pasta spends cooking in sauce help it absorb more flavor and finish cooking. This is also where the salted pasta water seasons your sauce.

variations on tomato sauce

"Red sauce" as it's often called, is an icon in the world of Italian-American food, a world I know well from my childhood in New Haven, Connecticut. But, while tomato sauce– aka *pomodoro* sauce, aka spaghetti with fresh tomatoes–is indeed found throughout Italy, red sauce is far too general of a term to cover all of the variations found around Italy. Each one has its own nuances that vary from kitchen to kitchen, grandmother to grandmother, chef to chef. No matter its name, I crave some version of it nightly. Each recipe included here is meant to represent a season so you can enjoy a homemade version of this essential sauce all year round. Whether made with canned tomatoes, or with summer's peak tomato bounty, I do not discriminate!

arrabbiata

makes about 4 cups

Arrabbiata sauce was one of the first things I learned to cook. My best friend taught me during my freshman year of college and I've never forgotten that moment. I have since tinkered and tweaked her recipe, but one thing remains: it's spicy! Over the years, my palate has taken a greater and greater liking to spicy dishes and this recipe is what I believe to be my greatest spicy tomato sauce yet, all made on a whim one night with the items I had lying around my kitchen, including tomato paste. It's an ingredient I don't use often, but here it adds depth and richness to the end result.

2	28-ounce cans San Marzano tomatoes
½ cup	olive oil
8	whole garlic cloves, plus 3 cloves thinly sliced
¼ cup	tomato paste
1 tablespoon	fennel seed
1 tablespoon	crushed red chili flakes
2 tablespoons	Calabrian chili paste
2 tablespoons	kosher salt
4	sprigs fresh oregano

1   Drain the tomatoes over a small bowl. Reserve the juices. Use your hands to break the tomatoes into pieces and place them in a bowl. Set both bowls aside.
2   In a large, wide pan over medium-low heat, warm the olive oil. Add the whole garlic cloves and cook until slightly golden brown, about 6 minutes. Stir in the sliced garlic and sauté until fragrant but without color, about 1 minute. Add the tomato paste and cook until it becomes a deep, rich color and has absorbed some of the oil, about 4 minutes.
3   Stir in the crushed tomatoes, half the reserved tomato juice, the fennel seed, and chili flakes and paste. Reduce the heat to low and simmer, stirring occasionally, until the sauce has reduced slightly, about 45 minutes.
4   Stir in the salt and oregano and cook 5 minutes. Remove the oregano sprigs. Taste and adjust seasoning if desired.

no-cook cherry tomato sauce

serves 4

When I buy cherry tomatoes at the market during the summer, I usually don't make it home without eating most of them—especially when I find a bunch of bright yellow Sun Golds. Most abundant in August and September, there really isn't any substitute for their candy-like sweetness. This sauce is a delicious way to integrate them, or any kind of sweet cherry tomato, into a quick seasonal meal. The preparation is simple: tomatoes are salted to release their juices, then infused with loads of dynamic flavor from the addition of pungent fresh herbs and citrus zests. For an irresistible snack, skip the pasta and serve the sauce over a thick slab of mozzarella with a hunk of crusty bread on the side.

3 pints	cherry tomatoes, preferably Sun Gold
2 tablespoons	kosher salt
3	garlic cloves, chopped
	zest of 1 lemon
	zest of ½ orange
1½ tablespoons	crushed red chili flakes
½ cup	olive oil
2	sprigs basil, leaves only, torn
3	sprigs marjoram, leaves only
3	sprigs mint, leaves only, torn

1   Halve the tomatoes and place them in a large mixing bowl. Add the salt, gently toss, then let sit for 1 minute. Add the garlic, citrus zest, chili flakes, and olive oil, and stir gently to combine. Set aside to marinate for 20–30 minutes.
2   Let the sauce sit at room temperature until ready to use. Add the basil, marjoram, and mint right before cooking the pasta (if using) so they stay fresh, but still have time to add flavor. The heat of the pasta will warm the sauce.

no-cook cherry tomato sauce
pg 113

30 clove sauce

I'm obsessed with garlic. Garlic and tomatoes together? Even better. This recipe was born out of my desire to create a sauce that highlighted garlic in all of its glory. I can't remember how on earth I came to the conclusion that thirty was the ideal number of cloves, but now it's written in stone and part of my repertoire. (If you don't want to count out thirty cloves exactly, just use what would normally be an outrageous amount of garlic and you should be covered.) When you see the thirty cloves actually laid out in front of you, don't get nervous and start second-guessing—the garlic is cooked very slowly, which brings out its inherent sweetness. I like to leave some of the cloves whole so that I discover them like surprise gifts at random bites while I eat.

1 cup	olive oil
30	garlic cloves (about 2 large heads)
3	28-ounce cans San Marzano tomatoes
2 tablespoons	fennel seeds
½ tablespoon	crushed red chili flakes
3	sprigs basil
1½ tablespoons	kosher salt

1   In a large, heavy saucepan over medium-low heat, warm the olive oil. Add the garlic and cook until softened and it begins to caramelize to a golden color.

2   While the garlic cooks, use a colander to drain the tomatoes over a small bowl. Reserve the juice. Use your hands to squeeze and crush the tomatoes.

3   Use the back of a fork to smash half of the garlic cloves in the pot. Stir in the crushed tomatoes, fennel seed, and chili flakes. Bring the mixture to a simmer and cook, stirring occasionally, until the flavors have melded and the sauce has thickened slightly, about 45 minutes.

4   Add the basil and salt and cook for 5 minutes. Remove the basil. Taste and adjust the seasoning if desired, but remember the pasta water will also season it further.

quick-cook summer tomato sauce

makes about 4 cups

This recipe is best in late summer when tomatoes are at their peak. It's also a tasty, dinner-time solution for sweltering nights when you can't stand the thought of turning on the oven. The hard part is peeling and seeding the tomatoes, but worth the effort. Experiment with different varieties from your garden or farmers market. As long as the tomatoes are ripe this sauce will be a winner every time. Serve it with your favorite pasta, torn basil leaves, and a drizzle of good-quality olive oil.

5 pounds	ripe plum tomatoes
½ cup	olive oil
10	garlic cloves, sliced
1 teaspoon	kosher salt

1   Bring a large pot of water to a boil. Fill a large bowl with ice water and set it aside.
2   Use a paring knife to make a small X in the core of each tomato. Place the tomatoes in the boiling water and blanch until their skins begin to peel away, about 10–15 seconds. Use a slotted spoon to quickly transfer each tomato to the ice bath to cool.
3   Peel the skin of each tomato, then halve it lengthwise and squeeze out and discard the seeds. Use your hands to crush the tomatoes, then place them in a bowl and set aside.
4   In a large, heavy pan over low heat, warm the olive oil and sliced garlic and sweat until fragrant but without color, about 2 minutes. Stir in the tomatoes and salt, then cook until the sauce reaches a simmer, about 20 minutes. Taste and adjust the seasoning if desired, but remember that the pasta water will also season it further.

mortar and pestle pesto with stracci

serves 4

There is nothing quite as satisfying as using traditional cooking methods like an old-school mortar and pestle. Crushing garlic, nuts, and basil by hand and watching as they transform into a paste brings you back to the real country cooking of Italy. No motors, no plugs; just time, effort, and stunning results. Pesto epitomizes summer, when basil is at its peak, and I look forward to it every year—it brings back fond memories of picking basil straight from my backyard garden in Connecticut. Here, I pair the pesto with homemade *stracci*—large sheets of fresh pasta—but it would work equally well with spaghetti, gnocchi, or virtually any pasta shape if you don't have time to make the fresh pasta. While any pasta shape will do, a food processor or blender really won't. So, if you don't have a mortar and pestle, get one.

for the pesto

2	cloves garlic
¼ cup	toasted pine nuts
1	large bunch basil, leaves only
½ cup	olive oil
¼ cup	grated Parmigiano-Reggiano
¼ cup	grated Pecorino Romano cheese
¾ teaspoon	kosher salt

1   Pound the garlic and pine nuts in the mortar and pestle. Add the basil leaves, a few at a time, and continue to pound with each addition. The basil will begin to break down and release its oil. Continue until all of the basil is added.

2   Gradually add the olive oil and grind until a paste is formed. Fold in the cheeses. Season and taste, adding more salt if necessary. Transfer to a large bowl, and set aside.

for the *stracci*

1 pound	00 flour
8 ounces	egg yolks (from roughly 10 large eggs)
	semolina flour
	fresh basil leaves and grated Pecorino Romano cheese for serving

1   Place the flour in the bowl of a stand mixer fit with the dough attachment. With the mixer set on low speed, gradually blend in the egg yolks, a few at a time. Continue to blend until the mixture pulls together into a smooth dough. If the dough seems too dry, add a few teaspoons of water. The dough should be bright yellow.

2   Turn the dough out onto a clean, lightly-floured surface. Knead by hand until a smooth ball is formed. Cover with plastic wrap and let rest 30 minutes. (If you aren't going to use the dough right away, wrap tightly in plastic wrap and refrigerate.)

3   Divide the dough into three equal portions. With a manual pasta roller or the pasta attachment on a stand mixer, run the first portion of pasta through the widest setting and roll out two times. Repeat rolling, working your way through each setting twice until you have a large, thin sheet of pasta that is almost transparent. Dust the dough with flour and set aside. Repeat the steps with the remaining portions of dough.

4   Cut each pasta sheet into 5-inch squares. Stack the pieces, dusting each with a touch of semolina and layering a piece of parchment paper between to prevent sticking.

for the pasta and finish

1 cup	pesto
1 pound	*stracci*
	grated Parmigiano-Reggiano
12	basil leaves

1   Bring a large pot of water to a boil and generously season with salt.

2   Put 1 cup of pesto in a mixing bowl that will be large enough to toss the pasta in. (I never put pesto on heat so it always remains bright and fresh.)

3   Place the pasta in the boiling water. Since it is fresh pasta and very thin, it will only take 30–60 seconds to cook. Use tongs or a spider to remove the stracci from the water to quickly transfer the pasta to the bowl of pesto. Add a ¼ cup of the pasta cooking water and toss the pesto and pasta together until each square is coated. If needed, loosen the sauce with a few more spoonfuls of pasta water. Taste and adjust the seasoning if desired.

4   To serve, evenly divide the pasta among four plates. Garnish each portion with the grated cheese and fresh torn basil leaves.

mortar and pestle pesto with stracci
pg 118

whole wheat spaghetti with broccoli
pg 122

whole wheat spaghetti with broccoli

serves 4

there are several things i love about this dish:

1   Whole wheat spaghetti is earthy and richer than its white counterpart, and yet supposedly slightly better for you than regular pasta. Foods that taste better are rarely also the "healthy" option.
2   Anchovies, because they make everything better.
3   I used to absolutely hate broccoli but when eaten like this, I learned to love it. But anything braised with anchovy, white wine, and garlic would taste amazing.

This recipe was conceived from a top-to-bottom pantry raid at my parents' home one night. It was a "What do you make when there is nothing around?" kind of moment. They had these ingredients and I came up with this pasta that, though definitely not revolutionary in concept, is now one of my happiest go-to meals.

¼ cup	olive oil
3	garlic cloves, chopped
1	can anchovies, drained and chopped
1½ tablespoons	crushed chili flakes
1	head broccoli, trimmed and cut into ¼-inch pieces
1 cup	white wine
1 pound	whole wheat spaghetti
1 tablespoon	butter
½ cup	grated Pecorino Romano cheese
	kosher salt
12	basil leaves

1   Bring a large pot of water to a boil and generously season with salt.
2   Meanwhile, in a large saucepan over low heat, warm the olive oil. Add the garlic and sweat it until fragrant but without color, about 1 minute. Stir in the anchovies and chili flakes and cook for another 1–2 minutes. Add the broccoli and sauté 1 minute.
3   Stir in the white wine. Bring to a simmer and cook until the mixture is reduced by half. Continue to cook until the broccoli is tender and bright green, about 5 minutes.
4   Place the spaghetti in the boiling water and cook until al dente, about 7–8 minutes.
5   Use tongs to transfer the spaghetti to the pan of broccoli. Add ½ cup of the pasta water and toss over medium-low heat for 2 minutes. Add the butter and continue tossing until well coated. Remove from heat and stir in ¼ cup of the cheese. Taste and adjust the seasoning with salt if desired.
6   To serve, evenly divide the pasta and sauce among four bowls. Top each portion with some of the remaining cheese and torn basil leaves.

cacio e pepe kugel

serves 6–8

One of the best parts of taking time off from work was getting to attend holiday functions with family and friends. I came up with this dish for a Yom Kippur breakfast; it takes my Jewish heritage and love for Italian food and combines them in a traditional kugel (essentially a noodle casserole) with the flavors of *cacio e pepe*, a traditional Roman spaghetti dish. The result is a super simple dish packed with tons of pepper and the creaminess of Pecorino, creating an indulgent comfort food from two cultures meeting in the middle.

2 pounds	ricotta, whipped in a food processor or stand mixer until smooth
1 pound	mascarpone
3 cups	Pecorino Romano cheese
1 teaspoon	kosher salt
2 tablespoons	freshly ground black pepper, plus more for garnish
1½ pounds	dried linguine, fettuccine, or spaghetti
1 tablespoon	butter

1   Heat the oven to 350°F. Bring a large pot of water to a boil and generously season with salt.
2   In a large mixing bowl, combine the ricotta, mascarpone, and 2 cups of the pecorino. Stir well to combine. Stir in the salt and black pepper.
3   Place the pasta in the water and cook until just barely al dente, about 6 minutes. (The pasta will finish cooking in the casserole.) Drain and transfer it to the seasoned cheese mixture, stirring to coat the pasta.
4   Grease a 9x13-inch baking dish with the butter. Transfer the pasta-cheese mixture to the baking dish and top with the remaining cheese. Bake until the top and sides are crispy and golden brown, about 35 minutes. Sprinkle with more black pepper for garnish, cut into squares, and serve.

cacio e pepe kugel
pg.123

fettuccini, zucchini, garlic scapes, and lemon
pg 126

fettuccini, zucchini, garlic scapes, and lemon

serves 4

In this dish, I use both garlic scapes and garlic bulbs. Garlic scapes are the stems and un-opened flowers of a garlic plant, and can be found during a very short window at the start of summer in New York City farmers' markets. They're rather unusual looking—coiled, green, and long—so it's understandable that most people don't know how to use them. You can use scapes in many of the same ways you would use garlic cloves; scapes offer a delicate, sweeter garlic flavor, while garlic cloves are more pungent. In this dish, I sauté both the scapes and cloves to achieve a balance and depth of garlic flavor. Adding the scapes at the end keeps them crunchy and bright, and builds textural dimension in the dish. Here, they're combined with zucchini, which is a great sponge for soaking up the flavors in a sauce.

4	small zucchini, julienned
1 pound	fettuccine
3 tablespoons	olive oil
10	cloves garlic, peeled and finely chopped
1½ teaspoons	crushed red chili flakes, plus more for garnish
1	bunch garlic scapes, thinly sliced
¼ cup	Pecorino Romano cheese, plus more for serving
	juice and zest of 1 lemon
	kosher salt
¼ cup	bread crumbs
4	sprigs mint, leaves only, torn
	freshly cracked black pepper

1   With a mandoline adjusted to a thick setting and fit with a medium julienne tool, slice the zucchini, avoiding the seedy core. Be sure to cut only the green meaty part, stopping on each side before you get to the seeds. Reserve the seedy core of the zucchini for another use.

2   Bring a large pot of water to a boil and season generously with salt. Place the pasta in the water and cook until al dente, about 7–8 minutes (2–3 minutes if using fresh pasta).

3   As the pasta cooks, warm the olive oil in a large sauté pan over low heat. Add the garlic and sweat until fragrant but without color, about 1 minute. Stir in the chili flakes.

4   Use tongs to transfer the pasta to the sauté pan. Add 1 cup pasta water, the garlic scapes, and zucchini. Toss over low heat for about 3–5 minutes, until the fettuccine has absorbed the sauce and the zucchini has softened slightly. Add the cheese and toss once more. If needed, add more pasta water to loosen the pasta.

5   Stir in the lemon juice and zest. Taste and adjust the seasoning with salt if desired. To serve, evenly divide the pasta among four bowls. Top each portion with bread crumbs, cheese, mint, cracked black pepper, and extra chili flakes.

spaghetti with ramps

serves 4

Ramps are the first spring vegetables and to me, there's nothing quite as exciting as when they begin to emerge. They have a short season of about six weeks and can be hard to find, making them highly coveted by chefs. They are wild leeks that can be used in any dish in place of onion, but their flavor is just so much more special than an onion. Their leafy green tops make a great pesto, while the white bulb end is terrific for vinaigrettes. But really, there is nothing better than a grilled ramp, simply tossed with olive oil and vinegar. This pasta dish is another one of my favorite ways to use them. It borrows from the idea of a basic *aglio e olio* (garlic and olive oil) and brings it to a new level. The result is a spicy, flavorful meal that's a welcome reminder that summer is on the way!

½ cup	olive oil
2 cups	sliced ramp bulbs, plus 1 cup roughly-chopped ramp greens
2	garlic cloves, thinly sliced
1 pound	spaghetti
1½ teaspoons	crushed red chili flakes
¼ cup	chopped parsley
	zest of 1 lemon
½ cup	grated Pecorino Romano cheese
	kosher salt
¼ cup	bread crumbs

1   Bring a large pot of water to a boil and generously season it with salt.

2   In a large saucepan over medium heat, warm the olive oil. Add the ramp bulbs and sweat them until tender but without color, about 5 minutes. Stir in the garlic, cook for 1 minute, then remove the pan from the heat.

3   Place the spaghetti in the boiling water and cook until al dente, about 7–8 minutes. Use tongs to transfer the spaghetti to the pan of cooked ramps and set over low heat. Add 1 cup pasta water and cook until the pasta has absorbed the liquid and the flavors in the sauce have melded, about 1–2 minutes. Add the ramp greens, chili flakes, parsley, and lemon zest. Toss to combine. If needed, add more pasta water to moisten the mixture.

4   Remove the pan from the heat and blend in ¼ cup cheese. Taste and season with salt if desired. To serve, evenly divide the spaghetti between four bowls and top each portion with a sprinkle of bread crumbs and the remaining cheese.

linguine with clams

I grew up in a kosher home devoid of shellfish, so my love for pasta with clams started later in life. This recipe screams summertime and makes me think of beach weekends spent shoving my face with steamers dipped in butter and lemon. Paired with linguine, they become a traditional pasta dish, and always a crowd favorite, but my take makes a vibrant detour with the addition of mint and lemon zest. The recipe also calls for removing the clams from their shells, which results in a more cohesive dish—and a less messy eating experience.

1 cup + 2 tablespoons	olive oil
5	cloves garlic, smashed, plus 2 cloves, finely chopped
3	dozen littleneck clams
1	bottle dry white wine
10	sprigs thyme
4 tablespoons	butter (½ stick)
1 pound	linguine
2 teaspoons	crushed red chili flakes
	juice and zest of 1 lemon
	kosher salt
3	sprigs of mint, leaves only
4 tablespoons	bread crumbs

for the clams

1 In a wide sauté pan over medium-high heat, warm the oil. Add the smashed garlic cloves and gently sauté until fragrant, about 1 minute.
2 Stir in the clams, wine, and thyme. As each clam opens use tongs to transfer it to a bowl.
3 Once all of the clams are cooked, use a fine mesh strainer to drain the cooking liquid into a medium bowl and reserve. Discard the solids.
4 Remove the meat from each clam and discard its shell. Chop half the meat, then place it, along with the whole pieces, in the reserved cooking liquid.

for the pasta and finish

1 Bring a large pot of water to a boil over high heat and generously season it with salt.
2 In a large sauté pan over medium-low heat, melt 3 tablespoons of butter. Add the remaining chopped garlic and sweat until fragrant, about 1 minute. Add 1 cup of the reserved clam liquid, and cook until reduced by one-third.
3 Place the pasta in the boiling water and cook until al dente, about 7–8 minutes.
4 While the pasta cooks, add the clam meat to the pan and warm through over low heat. Stir in the chili flakes. Use tongs to transfer the cooked pasta to the pan. Add ½ cup pasta water and toss until the sauce is mostly absorbed, about 1 minute. Add the remaining tablespoon butter and continue to toss. (The butter will add an element of richness and a sheen to the dish.) If the pasta tightens up, add some of the reserved clam liquid or more pasta water to moisten the mixture.
5 Just before plating, squeeze the lemon juice over the pasta. Taste and season with salt if desired. To serve, evenly divide the pasta among four bowls. Garnish each portion with mint leaves, lemon zest, and bread crumbs.

fettuccine, butter, truffles

serves 4

October means truffles and no one gets more excited for our first delivery of white truffles than me. People say they are too expensive, over the top, a luxury—I agree. But, I also know that they are so unique, with such incomparable flavor and fragrance that they are worth the hype. And since their intoxicating aroma is just as important as their delicate, nutty taste, it is best to shave them at just the moment before eating. If you are lucky enough to get your hands on one, I believe this preparation is the the best possible way to eat them: over fresh pasta with butter and Parmigiano-Reggiano. No more, no less. Treat yourself. You won't regret it.

1 pound	fresh pasta dough (page 118)
6 tablespoons	butter
½ cup20 grams	pasta cooking water
½ cup	white truffle (or more if you like)
	finely grated Parmigiano-Reggiano
	kosher salt

1　Using a pasta rolling machine or KitchenAid attachment, roll out the pasta dough and cut into fettuccine.
2　Bring a large pot of salted water to a boil.
3　Drop the pasta into the water to cook, it should only take 2–3 minutes, depending on its thickness. (Since it is fresh, it will cook very quickly.)
4　As the pasta cooks, melt the butter in a large sauté pan. Add about ¼ cup of the pasta cooking water.
5　When the pasta is cooked, use tongs to transfer it to the melted butter. Toss the pasta for 30 seconds–1 minute, until it is well coated and the sauce is absorbed. Remove from the heat and add half of the grated cheese. Toss to combine.
6　Divide the pasta between four bowls and top with the remaining cheese. Use a truffle shaver to shave the truffles paper thin over the pasta. You can do this table-side to give your family or guests the full sensory experience of the truffles!

turkey bolognese

Bolognese sauce is a classic Italian *ragu* typically made with ground pork, veal, and beef. It's usually considered to be rather rich, so when I began my quest to eat healthier, I also started making it with ground turkey. While turkey doesn't have the same fattiness and bold flavor as other meats, it still serves as a great vehicle to bring the flavors of the sauce together, and allows you to have a protein-rich meal while still getting your pasta fix. A good *soffritto* of fennel, celery, and onions is the key to building the flavors of this sauce, and the finish of nutmeg adds an unexpected wintery touch. I like to pair it with pappardelle, which provides generous surface area to absorb the sauce. Keep in mind that this recipe yields more than you need for one dinner so you can freeze it or keep in the refrigerator for a few days. Bolognese actually gets better after it has had time to sit, which allows the flavors to deepen.

for the bolognese

¾ **cup**	olive oil
2 pounds	ground turkey
1	bulb fennel, finely diced
3	stalks celery, peeled and finely diced
1	large onion, finely diced
2	garlic cloves, finely chopped
1 cup	white wine
1	small piece of Parmigiano-Reggiano rind
1 tablespoon	black peppercorns
3	sprigs thyme
1 cup	juice from a can of San Marzano tomatoes

1   Place a large, heavy-bottomed sauce pot over medium-high heat. Add half of the olive oil and all of the turkey. Cook the turkey until golden brown, approximately 5–8 minutes. Once browned, use a slotted spoon to remove it from the pan and set aside.

2   Reduce the heat to low and warm the remaining 6 tablespoons olive oil. Add the fennel, celery, and onion, and slowly sweat the vegetables, until tender but without color, about 6–8 minutes. Add the garlic and cook 1 minute more.

3   Return the turkey to the pot and add the white wine. Simmer until the wine is almost evaporated. Meanwhile, use cheesecloth and cooking twine to bundle the cheese rind, peppercorns and thyme. Add the sachet to the pot.

4   Stir in the tomato juice and add enough water to cover all the ingredients. Simmer the sauce over medium-low heat for 1 hour to let the flavors meld. Remove from heat and discard the sachet.

for the pasta and finish

1 pound	pappardelle
2 cups	Turkey Bolognese
¼ piece	whole nutmeg, plus more for garnish
½ cup	grated cheese
	kosher salt

1   Bring a large pot of water to a boil and season generously with salt. Place the pasta in the boiling water and cook for 1–2 minutes if using fresh pasta, or until al dente for dried.

2   In a large pan, heat 2 cups of the sauce. Use tongs to transfer the cooked pappardelle to the pan. Add ¼ cup pasta water and cook until the sauce is absorbed, about 2 minutes. Grate the nutmeg into the pan.

3   Remove the pan from the heat and add half of the grated cheese. Taste and adjust the seasoning with salt if desired. To serve, divide the pasta and sauce among four bowls. Top each portion with the remaining cheese and, if you like, a bit more nutmeg.

turns out, i know nothing about asian food

Early on in my career I actually thought I wanted to cook Asian food, but eventually grew out of that when I realized that I was better at eating it than cooking it. My soul was Italian, not Vietnamese. Before my trip, I thought I understood what Thai and Vietnamese food were, but it didn't take very long to realize that I actually had no clue.

I first realized I knew zero about Vietnamese food when one of my friends told me my first stop had to be a bun cha shop in Hanoi and I didn't even know what bun cha was. When I learned how central to Vietnamese cuisine this was, I decided to go there immediately. After checking in to the hotel, I quickly navigated through the wild Hanoi streets, carefully dodging scooters which easily outnumbered walkers by 100 to 1. Crossing the street in this bustling city was no easy task, let alone when you're searching for what feels like a needle in a haystack, but I eventually found what I was looking for. The place was loud, crowded, and filled with locals—the kind of place in which, as a tourist, I definitely stood out, which I took as a good sign. I sat down, ordered beer and was served the house specialty: noodles, herbs, and grilled pork. The food was clean, light, and flavorful and yet still complex—layered with spice, herbs, and acid. This was not the five-ingredient cooking I was used to. If the rest of my days in Vietnam were to be filled with food like this, I was hooked. I went on to eat the typical noodle soup of the country, pho, daily. I gorged on more grilled pork and beef in different forms in different cities. I ate bahn mi. In Hue, a city famous for its fortress and also for its royal cuisine, the best dish I ate was in a dark, dingy space with no other diners: tiny, tiny clams, rice . . . and spice. It was rainy and depressing outside for the two days I was in that city, but it didn't kill my determination to get as many dishes as possible in per day. Where Hue was dreary, Hoi An was unexpectedly special. For such a small town, there is an insane food culture with countless native dishes from little rose-shaped dumplings filled with shrimp, to dishes made with thick noodles unique to Hoi An. There was a new discovery with each day I was there, every bite completely unfamiliar in the best way possible. It was a welcome challenge to try and figure out what was in the food I was eating, and it was so different from my own cooking style and flavors that it was completely transporting. An added bonus was that it felt like the food was good for me. It wasn't fatty and even though there were a lot of rice noodles, you are not eating a lot of refined wheat (i.e., PASTA), like I was back home. The food was filling but I never felt gross. I felt healthy. I even felt like I was losing weight, in spite of the fact that I was eating non-stop!

Since Thai food has always been a favorite of mine, I looked forward to sampling my go-to order: pad thai, fried tofu with peanut sauce, and whatever the name of that Thai stir-fried dish we get here is—the spicy one with chicken and chiles and basil. I think, like the Americanized Chinese food I grew up eating, these dishes, though they exist in Thailand, are not always at the forefront, which left room for me to discover so much more. This was such a surprise because going into the trip, Thailand had been the ultimate, the grand finale, the real place I had been eager to delve into since thoughts of the trip had been born. And although the cuisines of Vietnam and Thailand share so many ingredients, the cuisines are incredibly different. While I ate some truly special dishes throughout the islands of Thailand, I learned that you can't really count on the food of a first-class exotic resort. My food highlights in Thailand definitely came from Chiang Mai and Bangkok; in fact, some of my all time favorite food memories took place in those cities. Highlights included: incomparable fried chicken from a street vendor with sides of crispy skin, assorted curries, mango dipped in some dried chili concoction, cooked crab sold by the bag with a side of green chili dipping sauce in a food market, Northern Thai sausage piping hot off the grill, rotisserie chickens cooked over wood fires, and grilled bananas. The flavors were rich and intense and, in many cases, much heavier and greasier than the food in Vietnam. I loved the Thai food I ate, just not as much as I loved the food of Vietnam.

But on a trip like this, there doesn't have to be a winner. The foods of Thailand and Vietnam are distinctly regional and can differ even from city to city, from family to family. It's not so different from Italy in that way. What you eat in the south is so different from the north. What one town uses in a bahn mi is completely different from the next town. One town might be famous for a noodle dish and it could be nowhere to be found anywhere else. This realization drove my desire to hit as many places as possible, seeking out the most authentic regional specialties, eating as much as I could. They are both inspiring cuisines and amazing countries with equally rich culinary histories, just like Italy. I felt like I accomplished a lot in gaining an understanding of the basics in both places, but also know that I only uncovered the tip of the iceberg. Like Italian cuisine, it would take years of travel and study to truly understand the nuances of each country's food. Maybe in my spare time—in my next life.

Notes From a Food Tourist in Asia

1   Take probiotic pills daily before you leave and take them after every meal while there. I wasn't a believer, but I did it anyway because I was nervous about my sensitive stomach. They boost your immunity, which is important when introducing mass amounts of foreign foods into your body. It must have worked because I managed to escape with only minor discomfort. Best piece of travel advice ever given to me.

2   Focus on street food and not fancy restaurants, even if your norm is to seek out the finest in dining. You will get the most authentic food and flavor experiences by bouncing from street vendor to street vendor and casual eateries.

3   Regarding #1 & #2: Leave your fear at home. Often, you will not know what you are putting in your mouth. You will wonder how many hours it's going to take you to get sick. If you do get sick, you will spend hours doing a mental inventory of what it possibly could have been. You will never know. It will be worth it. I promise.

4   Many street vendors and casual food shops only serve one item—there is no menu. You hold up your fingers to show how many you want and the food appears.

5   By our over-sanitized standards, places you will eat will be dirty. There is a cultural tradition of throwing used paper napkins on the floor in Vietnam. You won't do it at first, but then you play along because you've stopped paying attention because the food is that good.

6   Drink lots of beer. It will keep you cool and it will make you believe you are killing any potential parasites. It also helps mellow out the high levels of spice in much of the food when water just won't cut it.

7   While eating, you will often sit on stools just 12 inches off the ground. It's part of the culture and not really comfortable, but after a while becomes second nature. So much so that I thought it would be cute to do something similar in the café at Lilia. No one liked it, except for me. The stools are now gone.

8   I can't believe I'm saying this, but Vietnamese coffee might be the best in the world—maybe better than the perfect Italian espresso. The secret is the condensed milk. Do not think about the calories. Just drink it, two to three times per day.

9   Like most countries, markets have the best finds. Not just for grocery shopping but for hidden stalls and vendors offering cooked dishes. Some of the best things I ate were nestled in the markets where locals shop.

10 Be a real tourist for a day and go on an organized food tour. You will get to see things and eat things you would have never ever found on your own, especially if you are on a limited time schedule in a big city.

asian diversions

The recipes in the following chapter are my tribute to Thailand and Vietnam. They are my way of preserving amazing food and travel memories. I tried to replicate the flavors as accurately as I could without having any idea what was in most of the food I ate. Same goes for the techniques, but in no way would I dream or claim that they are totally authentic. I studied, I tasted, I jogged my mental records, I flipped through my many, many photos, and I created my own versions of the traditional foods I adored. I hope that when you cook them, they introduce you or bring you back to these special places that, certainly from a culinary perspective, are truly electrifying.

"same same but different" green curry, chicken, eggplant

serves 4

Sometimes the fanciest hotel in the world does not deliver on food the way that the little shack down on the beach does. Such was the case while I stayed on the tiny Thai island of Ko Lanta. Four nights in a mellow paradise was a much needed reprieve from the hustle of navigating large Vietnamese cities, and the resort could not have been more amazing, but the Westernized version of Thai food they were serving was a complete disappointment: expensive and bland. So I strolled down the beach and 100 meters away found Same Same But Different, an outdoor beach restaurant where I happily ate lunch and dinner for the next three days. It was hot, sweaty, and overrun with flies, but it was constantly busy, full of big groups of international travelers. I couldn't have cared less about the environment because the flavors coming out of that kitchen were of the intensity we were expecting and had been looking for. Creating this recipe, inspired by that restaurant, has allowed me bring back those flavors and feel like I'm on that Thai beach again every time I eat it.

for the green curry paste

1	stalk lemongrass, chopped
2 ounces	ginger, peeled (about ½ cup)
3 ounces	chopped shallot (about ¾ cup)
4	garlic cloves
1	bunch cilantro, stems and leaves
10–20	green Thai bird's eye chiles, roughly chopped
4	kaffir lime leaves
1 teaspoon	coriander seeds
½ teaspoon	black peppercorns
1 teaspoon	kosher salt
1 tablespoon	palm sugar

Combine all the ingredients in the bowl of a food processor or a blender. Puree until you achieve a smooth paste. Set aside.

for the chicken and eggplant

4–6	chicken thighs
	kosher salt
	black pepper
6 tablespoons	olive oil
2	Japanese eggplants, split in half lengthwise and halved again (or 12 Thai green eggplants halved crosswise if you can find them)

1   Heat your oven to 375°F.
2   Season the chicken with salt and pepper and coat with 3 tablespoons of the olive oil. Roast in the oven until cooked through, 20–30 minutes.
3   Remove from the oven and set aside. Once cool enough to safely handle, use your hands to remove and discard the skin, and pull the meat from the bone, in large chunks. Set aside.
4   Heat a sauté pan over medium heat. Add the remaining 3 tablespoons olive oil and the eggplant flesh side down. Turn the heat down to low and cook slowly for until golden and tender, about 8–10 minutes. Remove the eggplant from the pan and cut into 3–4-inch pieces. Set aside as you finish the curry sauce.

for the finish

1 teaspoon	canola oil
3 tablespoons	green curry paste
12 ounces	coconut milk
1 tablespoon	tamarind paste
	juice of half a lime, plus more to taste
10	Thai basil leaves
¼ cup	cilantro leaves

1   Heat the canola oil in a small saucepan and add the curry paste. Sauté gently for about 2 minutes, stirring constantly, to bloom the aromas.
2   Add the coconut milk and whisk or stir to combine.
3   Add the tamarind and lime juice. Stir to combine.
4   Place the cooked chicken and eggplant in the sauce and cook just to warm through, 2–3 minutes.
5   Transfer to serving bowls and garnish with the Thai basil and cilantro leaves.

"same same but different" green curry, chicken, eggplant
pg 136

grilled squid, lemongrass, chiles, garlic
pg 141

bangkok fish dinner

makes ½ cup each

Deep in the heart of Bangkok's bustling Chinatown, where the smells of street food linger from dawn until dusk, there are two families that set up outdoor restaurants at four p.m. each day. If you're wise to the popularity of these places, you know that the lines start to form at three. The kitchen equipment finds a place on the sidewalk next to long stainless steel tables and little stools. Once you get a seat, you are given a number and, eventually, amongst the chaos of hundreds of sweaty, eager diners, someone will come take your order, which you've chosen from the pictures of seafood delicacies that fill the menu. Items range from crabs to clams to prawns to whole fish, all of which are simply grilled or stir fried and served with traditional sides of green (*Nam Pla Prik*) and red chili (*Prik Namsom*) sauces. Everything is washed down with cold Thai beer. In order to reenact this uniquely Thai experience, all you need to know is how to make those two quintessential sauces and then throw your choice of fish on the grill. Pick your favorites—whole fish, shrimp, squid—or whatever is fresh; season it with salt and pepper before grilling, have these sauces on hand for when they're done, and you will feel like you have traveled to another land.

green chili sauce

1 tablespoon	chopped shallot
1	clove chopped garlic
12	green Thai chiles, chopped
7 tablespoons	fish sauce
¼ cup	lime juice

1 Combine everything except the lime juice in a blender or food processor and pulse until finely minced and blended.
2 Transfer to a bowl and mix in the lime juice.

red chili sauce

½ cup	roughly chopped red Thai chiles
2 teaspoons	palm sugar
½ teaspoon	kosher salt
2 tablespoons	roughly chopped garlic
¼ cup	rice vinegar

Combine the chiles, sugar, salt, and garlic in a blender or food processor and blend to mince finely. Add the vinegar, pulsing to combine.

grilled squid, lemongrass, chiles, garlic   serves 4

This was one of my favorite dishes in all of my Southeast Asian travels and I ate it in an unassuming Vietnamese bistro-style restaurant in the food haven of Hoi An. This is my reinterpretation of the flavors that are still so vivid in my memory, and, surprisingly, not so far off from some of the Italian dishes I cook regularly—minus the lemongrass.

4 tablespoons	garlic, minced
¼ cup	lemongrass, tough outer leaves removed, finely chopped
	juice and zest of 2 limes
15	grinds black pepper
6 tablespoons	canola oil
1 pound	squid, cleaned of outside membrane
	kosher salt
2	serrano peppers, thinly sliced

1   Combine the garlic, lemongrass, half the lime zest, black pepper, and 4 tablespoons canola oil in a small bowl.
2   Place the squid in a mixing bowl or dish and add half the marinade. Let the squid marinate for at least 30 minutes.
3   Preheat your grill to high.
4   Pat the squid dry with paper towels. Coat the squid with the remaining 2 tablespoons canola oil and season with salt.
5   Place the squid on the grill and cook for 2 minutes before turning to cook for another 1–2 minutes. (You can place a pan on top of the squid as they cook to help them remain flat on the grill.) You are looking for them to be tender with nice grill marks, but squid of this nature should always cook quickly in order to avoid it becoming tough.
6   Remove the squid from the grill and toss with the remaining marinade.
7   Transfer to a serving platter. Drizzle the lime juice over the top and scatter the remaining lime zest. Garnish with the sliced serrano peppers.

bangkok fish dinner
pg 140

crab, curry, onions

serves 4–6

After seven relaxing days in the Thai islands, I ventured north to Chiang Mai to begin yet another eating adventure. At times, I found it tough to get my bearings in each new city, especially with language barriers and the chaos of thousands of people traipsing through the streets. So, sometimes I just had to randomly try my luck at a restaurant that I knew nothing about. You win some and you lose some. This recipe is inspired by one particular evening when I rolled the dice and picked a very large, open-air fish house—one of many in Thailand. That night, the random pick worked out in my favor because I had a crab curry that I'll never forget. It was spicy, fragrant, full of depth, messy in a good way; the kind of dish you don't want to end. I realized that this is an innovative way to use in-season soft shell crabs, which is how I love to make this, but you can also use picked crab meat, Dungeness, King crab legs, or even stone crabs if you want some luxury in your life.

for the thai curry powder

1 tablespoon	black peppercorns
2 teaspoons	white peppercorns
1 teaspoon	whole cloves
3 tablespoons	coriander seeds
1 tablespoon	cumin seeds
2 tablespoons	fennel seeds
10	cardamom pods
3 tablespoons	chili flakes
4 tablespoons	ground turmeric

1. Place all the spices except the turmeric in a dry sauté pan over low heat and toast only until aromatic, about 30 seconds to 1 minute.
2. Transfer the toasted spices to a spice grinder or high-speed blender and grind until you have a fine powder.
3. Place in a bowl and combine with the turmeric. Set aside.

for the crab curry

⅓ cup + 3 tablespoons	canola oil
1	large onion, thinly sliced into half-moons
3	garlic cloves, thinly sliced
2 tablespoons	grated fresh ginger
1	kaffir lime leaf
3 tablespoons	Thai curry powder
1 cup	coconut milk
1 teaspoon	kosher salt, plus more to taste
2 cups	rice flour
8	soft shell crabs
2	green Thai chiles, thinly sliced
3	eggs, beaten
3	green onions, tops only, thinly cut on a bias
	juice of 1 lime

1   Heat a pan over high heat and add 3 tablespoons of the canola oil.
2   Add the sliced onions and sauté quickly on high heat until they've softened but before they take on color, about 2–3 minutes. Turn the heat down to low and add the garlic, ginger, and lime leaf. Sauté for another minute.
3   Add the curry powder and stir until well mixed.
4   Add the coconut milk and increase the heat to medium-low. Cook for 5–8 minutes until the flavors are well blended.
5   Season with the salt, stir to incorporate, and remove from the heat. Set aside.
6   Place the rice flour in a bowl and coat the soft shell crabs in the flour, patting to remove excess flour.
7   Heat a large sauté pan over high heat and add the remaining ⅓ cup canola oil.
8   Gently place four of the crabs in the oil and cook until crispy, for about 1–2 minutes on each side. Remove from the pan and repeat with the remaining crabs. Reserve the cooked crabs on the side.
9   Place the curry mixture back on low heat and add the green chiles.
10 Add the eggs and cook gently, stirring, until the eggs are cooked to a soft scramble.
11 Cut the crispy crabs in half, vertically, and add them to the sauce to warm through. Once hot, transfer the crabs and curry to a large serving dish.

pork belly banh mi

serves 4–8

Since I'm not a huge sandwich eater, I wasn't a big fan of banh mi before I went to Asia. I had a chance encounter in Hoi An that changed that. After checking into my hotel, I decided to take a walk, quickly got lost, and ended up on a very residential side street. With no foot traffic, it was the last street you would ever imagine to have street food on it, but, like a mirage in the desert, in the middle of this desolate street were this little old lady and her little hibachi grill. Above the grill, encased in glass, were the neatly lined-up components of the banh mi sandwiches she was selling. The roll of pork. The chili sauce. The vegetables. The herbs. I had to have one and it was amazing. In that moment, I was completely sold on banh mi. What I loved best about hers was that, instead of often-traditional paté, she used a roasted pork belly rolled into a spiral like a traditional Italian *porchetta*. Our chance encounter on this empty street made it seem as if that lady and her banh mi were there just in that moment, just for me. Her banh mi was so delicious that whenever I hear someone is going to Vietnam, I send them to find her.

for the pork (makes enough for 8 sandwiches)

	zest of 1 orange
2	garlic cloves, grated
½	lemongrass stalk, grated
3½ pound	piece of pork belly, skin off
1 teaspoon	dried chili flakes
1 tablespoon	ground black pepper
1 tablespoon	coriander, coarsely ground
1 teaspoon	garlic powder
2½ tablespoons	kosher salt

1 Combine the orange zest, garlic, and lemongrass in a bowl and mix together. Place the pork belly, meat side up, on a tray or dish and rub the mixture all over it.

2 Combine the remaining spices and salt in a small bowl and mix well to combine. Use this spice mixture to evenly season both sides of the meat.

3 Cover and place in the refrigerator to cure overnight. (If you do not have enough time to do this, you can leave the pork at room temperature for 1–2 hours to cure, but overnight will allow the seasoning to penetrate for even more flavor.)

4 Preheat the oven to 375°F. While preheating the oven, remove the pork belly from the refrigerator and allow it to come up to room temperature.

5 Place the pork belly in the oven fat side up and cook, uncovered, for approximately 1 hour until golden.

6 After 1 hour, turn the oven down to 300°F.

7 Cook for another 2½–3 hours, or until tender, but not completely falling apart.

8 Remove the pork from the oven and let cool slightly if you are going to use right away. (If making for future use you can cool it down completely.)

9 When cool enough to do so, slice the pork belly into ¼-inch slices and set aside.

for the quick pickled carrots

1½ cups	white wine vinegar
2 cups	water
½ teaspoon	chili flakes
1 teaspoon	fennel seeds
1 teaspoon	black peppercorn
1	piece star anise
1 tablespoon	kosher salt
½ cup	sugar in the raw
2	garlic cloves, peeled
6	medium carrots, peeled

1   Combine all the ingredients, except for the carrots, in a small saucepan and bring to a simmer over medium-low heat. Remove from the heat and let it sit until cool. (Cooling the liquid will result in a cold pickle, which will keep the carrots crunchy.)
2   While the pickling liquid is infusing and cooling, slice the carrots into ⅛-inch-thick strips on a mandoline.
3   Place the carrots in a bowl and pour the cooled pickling liquid through a fine sieve over them. Allow the carrots to sit in the liquid for a minimum of 1 hour. The longer they sit, the more pickle flavor they will absorb. The pickled carrots can be stored in the liquid in the refrigerator for 2 weeks.

for the assembly (for four sandwiches)

16	slices pork belly
4	Vietnamese-style baguettes or French baguettes cut into 8-inch lengths
8 tablespoons	Vietnamese-style chili garlic sauce (Tuong Ot Toi Viet-Nam is a delicious brand and easy to find in stores or online)
1	seedless cucumber, thinly sliced
	pickled carrots
½	bunch of cilantro, leaves only
½	bunch of mint, leaves only
1	serrano chili, sliced

1   Heat a large sauté pan over medium heat and place the slices of pork in the pan to crisp to golden on both sides. If your pan is too small to do this all at once, you can do it in batches. Just lay the finished pieces on a platter while cooking the remainder. (This crisping of the pork will add an additional layer of texture to your sandwich and make it feel less fatty.)
2   Cut a lengthwise slit in the baguettes to open them out and toast lightly in a toaster oven or regular oven.
3   Spread a tablespoon of the chili sauce on the bottom half of each piece of bread. Layer each with slices of pork, followed by cucumbers, pickled carrots, herbs and chiles. (You can change this up depending on personal preference.)
4   Spoon another tablespoon of the chili sauce on top. Close the sandwich.

spicy green papaya salad
pg 150

spicy green papaya salad

Traveling through the streets of Vietnam, you find versions of this salad everywhere. Since I have always loved this dish in restaurants at home, it was exciting to sample it at its source. As you wander around, you can find street vendors making fairly straight-forward versions, or even some getting creative with add-ins like dried liver or beef jerky (the latter is quite addictive). For this version I kept it as simple as possible, but feel free to adorn it as you please. The green papaya, which is simply unripe papaya, can be quite bitter, so it's important not to skip the step of mixing it with salt and sugar and then squeezing out the liquid.

1	green papaya
1½ tablespoons	kosher salt
5 tablespoons	palm sugar
	juice of 4 limes
3 tablespoons	fish sauce
2	shallots, very thinly sliced
3	Thai red chiles, thinly sliced
¼ cup	cilantro leaves
¼ cup	roasted peanuts, chopped

1   Peel the papaya, cut it in half, and scoop out the seeds. Cut the papaya into quarters and shred each on the julienne attachment of a mandoline. Soak the julienned papaya in ice water for 20–30 minutes.
2   Transfer the papaya to a colander along with the salt and 1 tablespoon palm sugar. Massage the papaya so that the salt and sugar coat it and spread throughout. Let sit for 10 minutes, then use your hands to squeeze out any excess liquid. Set the fruit aside in a mixing bowl.
3   In a small bowl, combine the lime juice, fish sauce, and remaining ¼ cup palm sugar and mix well.
4   Add the dressing to the papaya, along with the shallots, and chiles.
5   Transfer to a serving bowl and garnish with the cilantro leaves and peanuts.

grilled prawns with tamarind

serves 4

Shrimp is not something I love or crave, but I know many people do. This dish, eaten in a dingy little restaurant in Vietnam's Ho Chi Min City, was a welcome burst of unfamiliar flavors. While I've had plenty of dishes that involved tamarind, I can't remember ever having one that was completely centered around its unique taste of sweet and sour, with the acidity reminiscent of citrus. If you don't know by now, acid and citrus are my thing, so I fell hard for this tamarind shrimp dish in Vietnam. Shrimp and prawns are typically categorized by how many make up a pound: u10s will give you ten in a pound, u16/20s will give you 16–20 in a pound, etc. For this recipe, u10s are ideal, but use the largest you can find.

3	garlic cloves, minced
	zest of 2 limes
2	lemongrass stalks, grated
1 teaspoon	ground chili flakes
2 tablespoons	black peppercorns, coarsely ground, plus more for finishing
3 tablespoons	canola oil
16	large prawns, preferably head on (if you can get u10's, great)
	kosher salt
⅓ cup	tamarind paste, plus more for finishing
5	scallions, greens only, cut into 1-inch lengths

1   Combine the garlic, lime zest, lemongrass, chili flakes, and black pepper in a bowl. Add the canola oil and mix to form a paste.

2   Peel and devein the prawns, leaving the heads on if applicable, and gently place into a bowl.

3   Gently toss with the garlic and lemongrass mixture so that the heads don't fall off, and marinate for at least 30 minutes.

4   Heat your grill to high. Season the marinated prawns with salt before placing them on the grill. Cook for 1–2 minutes per side, until just cooked through.

5   Individually transfer the prawns to a plate and immediately use a pastry brush to coat each with the tamarind paste.

6   Pile the prawns high on a platter and drizzle with a little extra tamarind. Garnish with the chopped scallions and more freshly ground black pepper.

grilled pork, hoi an style

serves 4–6

In spite of how touristy it is, Hoi An is still a pretty sleepy town; and it's also a truly inspiring food city. It clearly made an impression on my palate. Three or four of the recipes in this chapter are influenced from this tiny town of Vietnamese delicacies. I got this dish in a little restaurant tucked away in a nondescript alley. I usually try not to go to places that are praised in every guidebook, but the descriptions for this spot were just too good to pass up. I'm glad I broke my rule because it turned out to be one of the most special meals of my trip. No menu, no choices, no decision making. My kind of afternoon. You are delivered grilled skewers of pork, rice paper, herbs, greens, cucumbers, pickled vegetables, spring rolls and, to top it all off, the most amazing rice flour crepes ever. So many flavors, so many textures, and because of the "make your own" nature of this dish, it's another great idea for dinner parties. While it is impossible to recreate the strange vibe of being in that random Vietnamese alley, I can sure try my best to recreate the food. (If you are averse to pork, this works great with chicken, too.)

for the crepes

2 cups	rice flour
¾ cup	cornstarch
3 teaspoons	ground turmeric
1 tablespoon	kosher salt
3½ cups	ice water
1 can	unsweetened coconut milk
1	egg
	canola oil

1   Mix together the rice flour and cornstarch in a large bowl. Add the turmeric and salt and mix to combine well.
2   While whisking, gradually add the ice water to the dry ingredients.
3   In a separate bowl, combine the coconut milk and egg and whisk to combine. Add to the batter, whisking again to fully incorporate. Set the batter aside to rest for at least 1 hour. Resting overnight is best.
4   Just before you cook the crepes, preheat your oven to its lowest setting to keep the crepes warm as you make them. Whisk the batter as it may have separated a bit while resting.
5   Heat an 8- or 9-inch nonstick pan over medium heat. Add 1 tablespoon canola oil.
6   Add 2½ ounces of batter to the pan, swirling it around to make sure it evenly coats the bottom of the pan in a thin layer. Cook until bubbly and crispy on one side, about 2 minutes, before flipping to cook on the other side. This is not your average crepe—it's ok to brown and crisp these a little.
7   Once cooked through, slide from the pan to an ovenproof plate or sheet pan and place in the oven to keep warm as you make the rest.

for the pork

1 tablespoon	black peppercorns
1 teaspoon	chili flakes
10	garlic cloves, smashed
3	shallots, chopped
½ cup	minced lemongrass
¼ cup	palm sugar
2 tablespoons	fish sauce
1 tablespoon	sesame oil
2 pounds	pork shoulder
	wooden skewers, soaked in water

1   In a mortar and pestle, combine the black peppercorns and chili flakes. Pound until they are crushed. Add the garlic, shallots, lemongrass, and palm sugar and continue to pound until a paste is formed. You want the paste to have a little texture; it shouldn't be completely smooth. You can also do this by pulsing in the bowl of a food processor.
2   Add the fish sauce and sesame oil and mix to combine.
3   Cut the pork shoulder into thin pieces approximately 4 inches long by 2 inches wide, and about ¼-inch thick.
4   Place the pork in a large dish or bowl and rub the marinade into the meat. Marinate for several hours (if possible, overnight is ideal), or at a minimum, 1 hour.
5   After marinating, skewer the meat onto the wooden skewers and set aside.
6   Preheat your grill to high. Once hot, place the skewers on the outside perimeter of the grill and cook for 3–5 minutes per side, until cooked through.

to serve

1	bunch cilantro
1	bunch Thai basil
1	bunch mint
½ cup	mustard greens and/or pea tendrils
1	seedless cucumber, peeled and sliced thinly, lengthwise, into ¼-inch thick strips
	pickled carrots (from pg 147)
1	package rice paper (plus warm water for softening)
	crepes
	Sambal chili sauce, for dipping

1   Clean and dry the herbs, and then arrange them, the mustard greens or pea tendrils, sliced cucumbers, pickled carrots, meat, and rice paper on various serving platters and vessels. Take a piece of softened rice paper and add a few pieces of meat and whatever combination of herbs and vegetables you like. Fold it up, wrap it in a crepe, dip it in the chili sauce, EAT!

pho – it's for breakfast

I learned three things about pho in Vietnam:
1. How to pronounce it correctly.
2. That you eat it for breakfast, not lunch or dinner like we assume stateside.
3. Finally, perhaps the most important lesson of all, if you don't get pho by 9 or 10 in the morning in Vietnam, then you're most likely not going to get it at all.

Pho is made by women who are basically cooking and serving it out of their homes. They make one perfect pot of pho for the day, and that's it. Once it's 86'd, that's all she wrote until the next day. I combined a couple of my pho memories to create this version. I know it might be hard to wrap your head around eating it for breakfast if you're not accustomed to such savory food in the early hours, but it's warming and filling and a great way to start the day. I won't blame you if you eat it for dinner though.

for the broth (makes 3 quarts)

2	small Spanish onions, halved
1	piece of ginger, 3-inches long
5	shallots
3 pounds	brisket
3½ tablespoons	kosher salt, plus more to taste
1 tablespoon	canola oil
5 pounds	beef bones (It can be a mixture of knuckle, marrow, neck, or any available beef bones at your local butcher.)
3	carrots, peeled and cut in to 1-inch chunks
1 tablespoon	black peppercorns
2	whole star anise
10	whole cloves
1	cinnamon stick
10	cardamom pods
1 tablespoon	coriander seeds
1 tablespoon	fennel seeds
2 tablespoons	fish sauce

1. Preheat the oven to 450°F.
2. With the skin intact, cut the onions in half and place them flesh side down in a large, heavy-bottomed, oven-safe sauté pan. Without peeling them, add the ginger and shallots. Place the pan in the preheated oven and roast until tender and browned on the outside, approximately 1 hour.
3. While the aromatics cook, season the brisket generously on both sides with 2 tablespoons salt and set aside for 1 hour.
4. Remove the browned aromatics from the pan. Set aside until cool enough to handle. Peel the skin from each and discard, reserving the flesh.
5. Heat a large sauté pan over medium-high heat. Add the canola oil and place the brisket in the pan. Cook for approximately 3–4 minutes on each side to achieve a golden brown crust. Remove the pan from the heat.

6   Transfer the seared brisket and the beef bones to a large stockpot. Cover with water (about 7 quarts). Over medium heat, slowly bring the pot to a simmer, occasionally skimming any impurities or oil from the top and discarding. Once the stock has come up to a simmer, turn the heat down slightly so it stays at a slow simmer. Be very careful not to boil.

7   Add the carrots and all the spices (not the fish sauce) along with the roasted onion, shallot, and ginger. Continue to cook over low heat for 5–6 hours, continuing to skim the excess oil and impurities as needed. After 5–6 hours, the broth should taste rich and meaty and the brisket should be fork tender.

8   Use tongs to remove the brisket from the stock and set aside.

9   Strain the stock through a fine sieve lined with cheesecloth or a cloth napkin. Season the broth to taste with approximately 1½ tablespoons of salt and the fish sauce. Taste and adjust with more seasoning if necessary.

to serve

1	jalapeno or serrano pepper, thinly sliced
1	red chile, thinly sliced
1	bunch scallions, thinly sliced
4	sprigs Thai basil
4	sprigs mint
4	sprigs cilantro
1	lime, cut into wedges
	Sriracha
1 pound	rice noodles (fresh or dried)
	pho broth
16	slices of brisket, cut into ¼-inch-thick pieces (Slices should be about 3-inches in length)

1   Line a large tray or serving dish with all the condiments. I like to lay the fresh herbs out and put the chiles, scallions, and limes in separate ramekins.

2   Cook the rice noodles according to package instructions.

3   Evenly divide the cooked noodles among four bowls. Place four slices of brisket on top of the noodles in each bowl. Pour the hot broth over the noodles and serve.

4   Allow each person to personalize their own pho with the herbs and garnishes.

yes, i'm free

Chefs never have long periods of truly free time. You have pockets that come in minutes, maybe a string of hours. You hope for one full day off, but when you get it, you are always mindful that you might get a random call to get into work ASAP because something went wrong, or a member of your brigade is a no show. You are lucky if you work in a restaurant that is closed one day a week so there is a guarantee of a break. Your schedule changes frequently. One week you are off on Monday, the next week it might be Thursday. There is very little regularity, especially when you are the low man on the totem pole and only rising up the ranks in the kitchen. When you do finally get one day off, you cherish it so much that often you are overwhelmed by all the possibilities of what you should do. You are often so paralyzed with choice that you do nothing. You literally waste your one day. On work days, social engagements consist of maybe fitting in coffee with a friend before rushing to work. In your twenties and thirties, you go out for drinks late into the night, usually with the people you work with. You miss holidays and constantly disappoint your family. Your friends don't understand why you never have time for them. Externally, you fight to convince the world that this is normal, this is what it takes to succeed in your industry and that anyone who is a cook or aspiring chef does the same thing. Your mentors are right by your side, working just as many hours. You respect them and want to be like them, so you keep pushing. But internally, there is a struggle that you never own up to because you don't want to appear weak. You want to be the first one in every morning, and the last one out after a grueling service. But somewhere inside, you know something is not right. This goes on for years. In my case, twenty of them.

By the time I was executive chef, I was working six days a week. Five-day weeks happened, but they were an all-too-rare exception. My team worked six days too, so we all lived in the same state of exhaustion. We had kitchens to run, the next dish to create, and important people to feed. We were always short staffed. It weighed on all of us. But the core group, whether they were devoted to me, or to themselves and their craft, stayed the course. For years, we were in it together. But we were all tired, all the time. And, probably, some of us even a little angry. I watched their relationships struggle and fail. I saw a lot of tears. I felt a guilty sense of responsibility. I felt like I was indirectly ruining their lives, even though they, like I, had chosen this profession. And I was right there with them, having my own issues. We had two restaurants to take care of. We were busy and challenged and thriving off it in many ways, and you could see that in our collective and individual growth. Still, I wanted desperately to create a better environment for me and my team and I didn't know how. So I controlled the only thing I could and changed my own environment. As a leader, I always wanted to be the pillar of strength for my team, which I had spent years building and making sure was a cohesive unit that could rely on me. Leaving them behind made me feel bad in many ways; it felt like abandonment, like I had let them down. And yet, here I was making this decision for me and only me. I had been consumed by taking care of other people in my kitchens for so long that even though I knew I was doing something selfish, I felt like it was about time that I did. And, ultimately, the elation I felt by deciding to take care of myself and my own needs overpowered any regret.

When you have lived in a world where time is so sacred, unlimited availability is foreign. When I left my job, availability was one of the only things I had. Twenty-four hours a day with absolutely no obligation to be anywhere. I was ecstatic. I felt a freedom I had never felt before. I felt normal, or at least what I imagined normal was supposed to feel like. Coffee dates became longer. Lunch dates were frequent. Dinners with friends were easily planned, around their busy schedules, not mine. I saw my parents more. I was present at holidays and parties. I could go to a wedding for more than the day of because I could actually go away for a weekend. I could plan long vacations. I was present. I wasn't thinking about my to-do list for the next day. I wasn't thinking about how tired I was. I was just thinking about how much I looked forward to my next Pilates session or what I might cook for dinner that night. I was a regular person. Not a chef.

But a lot of time is a double-edged sword. An entire day is a lot of time to fill and, surprisingly, it often felt lonely. I would go hours without talking to other people, which in a restaurant is NEVER the case. There, you are constantly surrounded by people, even at the moments when all you want is solitude. All of a sudden, I was alone with a lot of quiet. I didn't miss the grind of restaurants, but I was definitely missing the built-in social aspect that comes with them. Having a social life in the outside world, I quickly learned, takes a lot of effort. It doesn't just appear; you have to work at it—especially when you have been socially unaccounted for all those years. The reality was that *other* people were working. They might not have been busy working in kitchens, but they had places to go. Commitments that naturally spoke for their time: meetings for work, businesses to run, spouses to see, and kids to raise. I can't say I was ever really bored; I managed to entertain myself. But having unlimited private time was not ideal, either.

Even though I made the most of my new jobless life, as weeks turned into months, I realized I was not happy as a solitary person. I craved connections. After all, the very reason I had ever gotten into the restaurant business was to cook for guests and make them happy. As I searched for my new path with all this time on my hands, it was helpful to understand that I need to be surrounded by people. Maybe I had needed a break from being forcibly surrounded by so many people, so much of the time. The grass isn't always greener. Be careful what you wish for. I had what I thought I wanted—more time, more space, more quiet. But it still wasn't enough to make me feel complete. It was only one little part of the equation that, when it was all added up, gave me my real answer: balance.

the whole chicken

Chicken gets a bad rap. People think of it as a boring go-to, but it can be just the opposite: a champion of the kitchen, soulful, heartwarming, and comforting. It can be the life of the party, getting along with every other flavor and ingredient, always going with the flow no matter how you cook it: roasted, braised, fried, grilled, or stewed. Below are some dos and don'ts for the perfect chicken.

1   **DO** salt your chicken heavily. The best is to dry salt for a few hours, or even overnight, or to brine it in some sort of a solution that includes salt and whatever other spices you like.
2   **DO** marinate your chicken. Garlic, herbs, spices, and citrus all do wonders to make a boring bird sing.
3   **DON'T** reject dark meat. In this chef's opinion, chicken thighs are by far the best part of the bird. If you are a naysayer to dark meat, rethink that choice.
4   **DON'T** accept that dry chicken is the only chicken. Skinless, boneless breasts are a popular choice at home because they are healthy, low in fat, and cook quickly, but that's a blessing and a curse because they can also be dry. Use them for very specific applications like curries and stews that save them with a lot of flavorful sauce, or for quick cooking skewers on the grill.
5   **DON'T** let a fear of too much food be the reason you don't roast a whole chicken. The ways that a roasted chicken can be put to use are limitless: soups, curries, chilis, tacos, salads, stocks. A whole chicken is the gift that keeps on giving, from the fat to the livers to the meat to the bones.
6   **DO** embrace chicken fat. Everyone adores pork fat, but where's the love for chicken fat? Always save your roasted drippings and any fat that rises to the top while making chicken stock. It is a great way to leave no waste behind while also adding lots of flavor to other dishes, like my Schmaltzy Stuffing (pg 164) or Chicken Fat Potatoes (pg 165).

my best roasted chicken

serves 4–6

The best chicken I ever made was at my parents' house. For some reason, I decided that pouring a half bottle of olive oil to coat every crevice of the bird was a good idea. Along with tons of lemon, garlic, and herbs, I ended up producing one of the most tender, moist, crispy-skinned birds ever. What also set it apart was that my mother only buys kosher chicken, which essentially come seasoned. Buy kosher when you can, and you won't be disappointed. Cooking and eating this chicken has become my absolute favorite way to spend a Sunday night at home.

1	whole chicken (3½ pounds)
	kosher salt
1	head of garlic, split in half horizontally
4	onions, peeled and each cut into 6 wedges
1	halved lemon
	zest of 1 lemon peeled into large strips (no pith)
6	sprigs rosemary
10	sprigs thyme
6	sprigs marjoram
6	garlic cloves, peeled and split lengthwise in half
1½ cups	olive oil
2	large fennel bulbs, cut into ⅛-inch-thick wedges

1   Remove all the innards from the chicken and rinse it. Generously salt it and allow to sit for 30 minutes.
2   Preheat the oven to 475°F.
3   Place the split garlic, 3–4 wedges onion, the lemon halves, and half of the herbs inside the cavity of the chicken.
4   Use your hands to very gently loosen the skin from the flesh, creating little pockets without tearing the skin. Evenly distribute the strips of lemon zest, garlic cloves, and remaining herbs in the pockets throughout.
5   While holding the chicken upright, vertically, pour ¾ cup olive oil into the pockets. (It will seem like a lot, but trust me.)
6   Rub the remaining ¾ cup olive oil all over the outside skin of the chicken.
7   Scatter the remaining wedges of onion and the fennel on the bottom of a roasting pan and place the chicken on a roasting rack inside the pan. Place it in the oven. After 15 minutes, turn the oven down to 400°F and cook until the juices run clear and a meat thermometer reads 160°F, about 50 minutes. Remove from the oven and let rest for 10–15 minutes.
8   Transfer the caramelized fennel and onions from the roasting pan to a platter and place the chicken on top. Go to town ripping it apart.

super bowl five chili wings   serves 4

I am not a football fan, but who doesn't love a great Super Bowl party and the classic bar food that goes with it? I'll admit that wings are not the easiest things to make at home; they require frying, which can be messy, and eating this dish is also messy—make sure you have a lot of napkins on standby. My sauce mix combines four different types of chili sauces and dried chili flake to create a Buffalo-style wing with more nuance. The different chiles offer varying tastes and heat levels, making for a more exciting mix of flavors. Nothing goes better with these wings than very chilled beer!

1½–2 quarts	canola oil
1 cup	Sriracha
½ cup	Frank's RedHot
¼ cup	Valentina hot sauce
½ cup	Calabrian chili paste
2 tablespoons	ground chili flakes
¼ pound	butter
16	whole chicken wings (2½ pounds)
	kosher salt

1   Pour the canola oil into a wide, heavy-bottomed cast-iron pan over medium heat, making sure to leave enough room in the pan that it will not bubble over once the chicken is added. Heat the oil to 375°F, using a thermometer to gauge.

2   While waiting for the oil to come to temperature, combine all the hot sauces, chili paste, and ground chili flakes in a small pot over low heat. Melt the butter gently into the hot sauce mix. Once melted, stir to combine and keep the sauce warm over very low heat until the chicken is fried.

3   Working in 2 or 3 batches depending on the size of your pan, place the wings into the hot oil and fry the chicken until it is crispy and cooked all the way through, approximately 10 minutes. Once cooked, use a spider or tongs to transfer the wings to a large platter or sheet pan lined with paper towels and season with salt. Repeat until all the wings are cooked and seasoned.

4   Place the wings into a large mixing bowl and ladle the warm chili sauce into the bowl. Mix until the wings are well coated. Serve right in the mixing bowl or if you need to get fancy with your wings, transfer them to a platter before serving.

super bowl five chili wings
pg 161

schmaltzy stuffing
pg 164

schmaltzy stuffing

serves 6–8

Stuffing is another one of the classics in my mom's small but finely honed and perfected repertoire. Many people put sausage or oysters in their stuffing, but in my house it was schmaltz, or rendered chicken fat. I'd always wanted to master my mom's stuffing and I finally got the opportunity to recreate it for friends and family at Thanksgiving during my year off. But I managed to put my own stamp on it while sticking to her schmaltzy secret when I discovered that Martin's potato bread makes pre-made croutons for Thanksgiving. I think the best schmaltz comes off the top of chicken soup or stock, so, when you make the Chicken Soup on page 168 you definitely want to get rid of the foamy scum, but keep that glistening fat for this stuffing!

1	loaf potato bread (preferably, Martin's) or 1½ 12-ounce packages potato bread croutons
6 tablespoons	olive oil
1 cup	rendered chicken fat
2	onions, peeled and finely diced
1	fennel bulb, trimmed and cut into ⅛-inch dice
6	celery stalks, peeled and finely diced
10	garlic cloves, peeled and finely chopped
2¾ cups	chicken stock
½ cup	grated Pecorino Romano
½ cup	grated Parmigiano-Reggiano
½ tablespoon	garlic powder
1 tablespoon	fennel seeds
1 tablespoon	kosher salt
1	sprig rosemary, leaves only, roughly chopped
5	sprigs thyme, leaves only
5	sprigs marjoram, leaves only
1	sprig sage, leaves only, torn into small pieces

1   Preheat the oven to 250°F.
2   If you've found Martin's packaged potato bread croutons for stuffing, great. Otherwise, break up regular potato bread into roughly 1- to 2-inch chunks and scatter them in an even layer on a sheet tray or two. Place the bread in the oven for approximately 20 minutes until it is dry, but not browned or toasted. (You can also dry the bread overnight by leaving it out in the open air.) Transfer it to a large mixing bowl and set aside.
3   Heat a large sauté pan over medium heat and add the olive oil and chicken fat.
4   Add the onions, fennel, and celery (what I like to call white *soffritto*) and sweat until soft and translucent, approximately 20 minutes.
5   After about 10 minutes of cooking the white *soffritto*, add the garlic and continue cooking for another 10 minutes.
6   Preheat the oven to 450°F. Transfer the vegetables while still hot to the same bowl as the toasted bread. Add the stock to the bowl. (This was always one of the keys to my mom's stuffing—soft and moist, but crispy on top.)

7   Add the Pecorino, ¼ cup Parmigiano, garlic powder, fennel seeds, salt, and the herbs. Gently mix to incorporate.
8   Transfer the stuffing to a 9x13-inch casserole dish and top with the remaining ¼ cup Parmigiano. Place it in the oven and bake until the top is crispy and golden brown, approximately 30 minutes.
9. Remove the dish from the oven and set aside to cool and set for just a few minutes before serving.

chicken fat potatoes
serves 4–6

Cooking in chicken fat, or as it is traditionally called, schmaltz, is one of my favorite techniques. When you use the fat from making chicken stock, you get the same flavor profile of rich poultry and subtle herbs and vegetables, which benefits the potatoes in this dish. If you don't have enough fat from skimming your stock, you can easily find it at butcher shops and fancy grocery stores. These decadent potatoes are a great accompaniment to any meat or fish dish or your breakfast eggs.

8	Yukon Gold potatoes, peeled and cut into round slices just thicker than ¼-inch
1½ tablespoons	kosher salt
6 cups	rendered chicken fat
5	rosemary sprigs
10	garlic cloves, peeled

1   Preheat the oven to 350°F.
2   Place the potatoes in a large baking dish and salt them. Let them sit for 10 minutes.
3   Melt the chicken fat and pour it over the potatoes. Scatter the rosemary and garlic throughout the dish.
4   Cover with foil, place the dish in the oven, and cook until tender but not falling apart, about 35–45 minutes.
5   When you are ready, use a slotted spoon to serve the potatoes to drain them from the fat.

chicken fat potatoes
pg 165

chicken soup with ricotta dumplings
pg 168

chicken soup with ricotta dumplings

serves 4

I grew up on chicken soup and matzo balls. As much as Italian red sauce is my comfort food, so is the food of my true heritage and, in particular, this dish. As any kid probably says, my mom's chicken soup is the best: simple broth, no limp, overcooked vegetables floating around, and just the right amount of fat left behind. My version of chicken soup with matzo balls combines my Jewish and Italian souls, inspired by a meal I had at an idyllic inn outside of Parma, Antica Corte Pallavicina. Their soup elegantly combined ricotta dumplings—essentially gnocchi—chicken broth, and truffles. I add herbs and leave the truffles out to make a more approachable version, but still, this dish is not a quick, easy meal. This is a recipe for a lazy Sunday when you have time to let the soup simmer for hours and make gnocchi by hand. One thing to note about my chicken soup is I always wait until the last hour of cooking to add aromatics and vegetables so I can extract the most chicken flavor with just a slight vegetal background.

for the broth

1 whole chicken
2 carrots, peeled and cut into large chunks
2 onions, peeled and cut into large chunks
½ head celery, cut into large chunks
1 leek, cut into large pieces
½ bunch of parsley stems
1 fresh bay leaf
1 tablespoon black peppercorns

1   Remove all the innards from the chicken (Save the livers! See page 170), rinse it, and place it in a large stock pot. Cover with water so that it comes about 2–3 inches above the chicken. Turn on the burner to medium-low and slowly bring to a simmer, making sure to skim off and discard the foam that forms. Turn the heat down to low and cook for 4 hours, continuing to periodically skim the fat from the top. (Skimming is important because it will leave you with a clearer broth.) Reserve all the liquid fat for use in another dish.
2   Add the vegetables, herbs, and spices, and cook the broth for 1 hour.
3   Strain the liquid through a fine mesh strainer, discarding the vegetables and herbs. (Keep the chicken—it's tender and easy to use in another dish, like the Green Curry on page 136.)

for the ricotta dumplings

1¼ cup	ricotta (10.6 ounces)
2	eggs
1 cup	grated Parmigiano-Reggiano (3.5 ounces)
roughly ⅓ cup	fine semolina (1.85 ounces)
about ¾ cup	00 Flour, plus extra for dusting (3.4 ounces)
	kosher salt

1   Mix the ricotta, eggs, and Parmigiano in a large mixing bowl until well blended.
2   In a separate bowl, mix together the semolina and 00 flour.
3   Gradually combine the flour mixture with the wet ingredients by adding a little at a time and folding gently until well mixed. Do not overwork the dough or you will end up with lead dumplings.
4   Refrigerate for an hour. (This makes the dough easier to roll out.)
5   On a lightly floured work surface, grab a small handful of dough and gently roll into ropes that are about ½-inch diameter. If the dough is a little sticky dust it with more flour, being careful not to add too much or you will lose the light fluffy texture.
6   Once all the dough has been rolled into ropes, cut the ropes into 1-inch lengths.
7   Using a traditional wooden gnocchi board or a fork if you don't have one, roll each piece of dough down the board or back of the fork with your thumb, pressing gently to make an imprint. Continue until all of the gnocchi are formed.
8   Bring a large pot of water to a slow simmer and add enough salt so that it tastes like the ocean.
9   Place the gnocchi in the water and cook for 20–30 seconds after they float to the top. They should be light and airy.
10 If not using right away, arrange the gnocchi in one even layer on a lightly oiled tray and cool in the refrigerator.

for the finish

	chicken broth
	kosher salt
	blanched gnocchi
2 tablespoons	olive oil
¼ cup	grated Parmigiano-Reggiano
	a few fennel fronds, chopped
	freshly cracked black pepper

1   Heat the broth, and season with salt to taste. Evenly divide the gnocchi among four bowls. Pour the hot broth over the gnocchi. Drizzle with the olive oil.
2   Garnish with the grated Parmigiano-Reggiano, fennel fronds, and freshly cracked black pepper.

tuscan style chicken livers

serves 4–6

I always thought that the chopped liver my family served on Jewish holidays was gross. Then, while living in Italy many years ago, I encountered Tuscan-style chicken livers that had a ton of complexity and my liver opinions were forever changed. My version will make you almost forget that you are eating liver at all, and it is a great way to utilize every part of the chicken. You can easily buy chicken livers at the butcher or grocery store, or stockpile them in the freezer every time you have some left over from a whole chicken. Serve these with grilled or toasted country bread for an awesome start to a meal or a light dinner with a salad on the side.

1 pound	chicken livers, cleaned of any sinew
2–3 tablespoons	kosher salt, plus more to taste
¾ cup	olive oil
½ cup	vin santo or brandy
1	onion, peeled and cut into ¼-inch slices
2	garlic cloves, sliced
	zest of 2 lemons, 1 peeled into large pieces (no pith), the other finely zested
3 tablespoons	capers
	grilled or toasted country bread

1 Salt the livers, mixing well to ensure they are fully covered. Place in a colander or fine mesh strainer over a bowl for 30 minutes. This will season them, but will also drain some of the blood, which makes for a cleaner taste. Remove the livers from the strainer and pat dry on paper towels.

2 Place a large, flat-bottomed sauté pan (cast-iron works great here) over medium-high heat and add ¼ cup olive oil.

3 Add the chicken livers in a single layer and quickly sauté on both sides until caramelized and brown, but still rare, about 1 minute per side.

4 Deglaze the livers with the vin santo and cook for another 1–2 minutes, so that they are still pink in the middle, medium-rare. Remove the livers from the pan, along with the juices, and set aside.

5 Return the same pan to medium-low heat and add another ¼ cup olive oil along with the sliced onions. Cook slowly until the onions caramelize, adding the garlic and large pieces of lemon zest, after about 5 minutes. Cook in total for about 15–20 minutes.

6 Remove and discard the large pieces of lemon zest before combining the onions, capers, livers, and pan juices in the bowl of a food processor. Gently blend the liver and onion mixture, while drizzling in the remaining ¼ cup olive oil until mixed and still slightly rough. It does not need to be totally pureed.

7 Season to taste with salt and serve on toasted or grilled country bread with a bit of finely grated lemon zest on top.

french dressing chicken   serves 6–8

"Drench chicken in bottled French dressing and grill it until charred." Sounds questionable, but this was one of my favorite dishes when I was a kid, and it makes me so nostalgic for warm summer nights eating dinner on the deck. There is some mystery to what actually constitutes that bottled, orange "French" dressing. What exactly makes it French? Turns out, it's nothing—just a clever marketing term. One night, while doing a pantry raid for a quick dinner at my parents', I took a stab at replicating the bottled dressing of my youth, and came up with a chicken marinade that was almost an exact replica of the chicken I grew up devouring. This preparation is great served alongside a salad or my favorite, grilled onions.

2 cups	ketchup
½ cup	Dijon mustard
¼ cup	red wine vinegar
¼ cup	olive oil
2 tablespoons	garlic powder
1 tablespoon	onion powder
1 tablespoon	hot paprika
2 tablespoons	sweet paprika
15	grinds black pepper
2 tablespoons	honey
1 teaspoon	Worcestershire sauce
8–10	chicken thighs

1   Combine all the ingredients, except for the chicken, in a bowl. Whisk to thoroughly mix.
2   Pour over the chicken and let marinate for at least 30 minutes. Preheat your grill to medium.
3   Place the chicken, skin side down, on the grill and cook slowly until it begins to char.
4   Turn the grill down to low and turn the thighs over. Continue to cook until done, about 15–20 minutes.
5   Remove from the grill. Place on a platter and serve.

french dressing chicken
pg 171

polenta crusted fried chicken, fennel pollen, chiles
pg 174

polenta crusted fried chicken, fennel pollen, chiles

serves 4–6

Fried chicken is pure indulgence and joy, which is also how I would characterize the memory of when this recipe was born. During a laid-back and spontaneous afternoon hanging out with my then-neighbor, now business partner, Sean, we turned on the TV and saw that the esteemed chef, Sean Brock, happened to be making fried chicken on a show. This made us both really hungry and sent us immediately to the store to buy ingredients and make our own fried chicken dinner. This an ode to chef Sean, because his southern techniques are tried and true, but I deviate a little by adding my own flavors. I think he might approve because the result is still sweet, spicy, crunchy, and tender—all the things you want in a crispy bird.

for brining and marinating

1 gallon	water
1¼ cups	kosher salt
¾ cup	sugar
2 tablespoons	honey
5	green tea bags
1	whole chicken, broken down into 6 or 8 pieces
1 quart	buttermilk

1. Bring the water, salt, sugar, and honey to a boil. Add tea bags, turn the heat off, and let the tea steep for 10–15 minutes.
2. Cool the brine mixture down in an ice bath. Once cold, submerge the chicken parts, making sure they are fully covered. The chicken should sit in the brine for 45 minutes.
3. Remove the chicken from the brine and pat dry. Discard brine.
4. Cover the chicken with buttermilk and let sit for another 30 minutes.

for the dredge

4 cups	flour
1 cup	finely ground polenta
3 tablespoons	kosher salt
3 tablespoons	finely ground chili flakes
3 tablespoons	finely ground fennel seeds
1 tablespoon	paprika
2 cups	buttermilk

1 Combine all the dry ingredients in a bowl.
2 Remove one of the chicken pieces from the buttermilk, allowing the excess to run off before dredging it in the seasoned flour and polenta mix. Once coated transfer it to a sheet tray lined with parchment. Repeat until all the chicken is dredged and coated. Leave the sheet tray in the refrigerator, preferably overnight. If you're in a pinch, leave the chicken in the fridge for several hours.
3 Sift the remaining flour mix to get rid of any clumps and reserve it for just before frying.
4 Once the chicken has rested, dip each piece of chicken into the remaining buttermilk and dredge in the leftover seasoned flour for a second time—this time a very light coat. Set aside.

for the fry

2–3 cups	canola oil
2–3 cups	olive oil
2–3 cups	chicken schmaltz
	kosher salt
2 tablespoons	fennel pollen, for dusting
1 tablespoon	ground chili flakes, for dusting

1 Put an equal amount of the oils and chicken fat in a large heavy-bottomed cast-iron pan. (How much you need depends on whether you have a 12- or 15-inch pan; just be sure not to fill it so high that the fat will bubble over.) Slowly heat the fat to 350°F, using a thermometer to gauge.
2 Carefully add the chicken pieces skin side down, individually, so that they are in one layer in the pan. You may have to fry in batches depending on the size of your pan.
3 Depending on the sizes of your pieces, cooking times will vary. Fry each for approximately 8–10 minutes, or until it starts to get crispy and golden. Then use tongs to turn each piece over and repeat until it is completely cooked through. If it starts to get a little too dark, turn the oil down to 325°F.
4 Transfer the chicken from the pan to a sheet pan or plate lined with paper towels to drain. Season with a dusting of salt, fennel pollen, and chili flakes.

mid-life conundrum

When I left my job to do nothing, I knew I wanted something different and that my current situation was not the right long-term plan. I appreciated everything it afforded me for most of the five years I was there. It was a place to land in NYC, a place where I made a name for myself, and made a great living. I developed my own personal cooking style in those five years; it was the first time I cooked without the voice of someone above me. I mentored other up-and-coming chefs and built teams. I pushed myself very hard and I pushed my team very hard, maybe too hard at times. My mandate was to maintain Michelin stars and I would do anything to make that happen so as not to feel like a failure. I didn't want to fail my bosses, my team, or myself.

I had everything you should want in a chef job. Except happiness. I was tired all the time, I was in terrible shape. My body was breaking down. I was unhealthy, mentally and physically. But when I left, I couldn't just exchange one job for another. That's not what this was about. I wasn't even necessarily *sure* what it was about, I just knew it was time to go. By far it was the bravest and ballsiest thing I had ever done. Leaving a "good" job without a plan at forty-two years old? Who did I think I was? I wasn't sure. I think, above all, that's what I had to figure out.

My whole identity post-college was as a cook and chef. To most people, that's who I was. There were many moments when I thought it was cool; chefs get a lot of attention and I wasn't an exception. People from all facets of my life showered me with love just for being successful professionally. They would visit me at the restaurants. I loved it, but I wanted to be known for something in addition to my cooking skill. It seemed like no one else I knew was defined solely by their profession; it was a part of who they were, but they were also wives, husband, fathers, mothers, with other interests and hobbies and pursuits. My profession was so consuming that it's all I had become. I didn't feel complete, but I didn't know it until I had time to reflect during my mid-life sabbatical.

As I settled into my role as a civilian and started focusing on other facets of my life, somewhere along the way I think I just became Missy. Missy Robbins. Friend, girlfriend, daughter. Intelligent, funny, relaxed. While I was very busy evaluating what my next move would be, I was equally as focused on my health. Pilates was a priority. I was going to a private trainer three times a week, even though I couldn't comfortably afford it. I was going to physical therapy to fix my ankle and my shoulder. I was contemplating getting serious about losing weight. An active social life became a priority. Sleep, an essential. I was mellow—mellower than I had ever been. I rarely had to be anywhere, with the exception of the occasional meeting to try to find the right partner or the right "thing." It was such a relief to not have to talk about my job at every dinner, at every family event. Now I talked about Pilates and travel. It was liberating and refreshing, since for the previous twenty years cooking and the restaurant world was all anyone talked to me about. While it's flattering and nice to get noticed, it was often boring. And, I've realized, often boring for those closest to me who were frequently subjected to hearing the same stories and conversations over and over.

I was not quite mid-life, but quickly approaching. And I wasn't having a crisis, but more of a conundrum. I had worked my whole life with a goal of opening my own restaurant and I thought that would happen in my early thirties. But it didn't, and though I was sometimes frustrated that I hadn't yet achieved that milestone, I was generally happy with my career path and the skills I had gained from taking my time. Now, jobless and twelve years past that unachieved goal, I didn't even know if I wanted it anymore. I was really burnt out, I was tired of dealing with staffing issues and constantly trying to find people to fill positions. I was sick of feeling responsible for other people. It was taking the fun out of cooking and taking care of guests. I didn't know if I wanted that burden any longer. I didn't want to work fourteen-hour days. I wanted to be able to take normal vacations and, more importantly, normal days off. I wanted a healthy relationship. That isn't to say that I didn't love things about the restaurant industry, but I was no longer sure that the positive out weighed the negative. On the flip-side, I also knew that I would always feel like I missed out on something if I never opened my own restaurant. While hopes and dreams change over time, I just had this feeling that I would regret it if I didn't open my own place. If I didn't set my own rules and develop the kind of place I wanted instead of fitting into someone else's dream. I felt like this was my last opportunity. I was in my forties and it certainly wasn't going to get any easier.

My mind swirled. My marketable skill was running a kitchen in a restaurant, but I also had a fascination with getting involved with large food companies, or vendors. I made up fantasy jobs in my head, like being the person who goes and seeks out all the best olive oils in the world for high-profile markets. I knew those jobs existed in some form, but I was paralyzed when it came to finding them. And maybe deep down I knew I was destined to stay in the restaurant world, so I frankly didn't try that hard. I had an interest in opening something like the gourmet markets I had come to love as a kid, an Italian shop with fresh pasta to-go by day, and turn it into a private dining room at night where I could just cook for people as if they were in my home dining room. (I still want to do that.) The latter was the real dream, the one I could really visualize. But I wasn't sure there would be enough financial stability. While money was certainly not the most important thing in the world, I didn't want to go backwards. A Voce provided me with a financially comfortable, stable lifestyle and I didn't want to lose sight of that. I wanted to again make sure I could pay my bills and not worry about my bank account every time I went out to dinner. I also knew that I didn't really, truly want to work for anyone or take a big job just because it would pay me well.

I cherished all the meetings I had at different points throughout the year, and appreciated very high-profile people taking the time to meet with me, even if prospects were dead ends. Each meeting provided me with some sort of insight and got me closer to understanding what I wanted to do next, or more importantly, what I didn't want to do. The most pivotal of all was a meeting with Danny Meyer. He looked at me and said, "When are you happiest, with a pan in your hand?" It was at that very moment that I finally understood what my place should be. "NO," I quickly said, without even a thought. I was not happiest "just cooking." What made me happy was planning, creating, leading, mentoring, picking out china, looking at menu design. I wanted to be a chef, but I also wanted to be a restaurateur. I didn't want to be a "working chef" as we call ourselves. I didn't want to be the person doing production, I didn't want to be the person behind the line. I hadn't been that for years. But I thought in order to open my own place I might have to become that person again. I wrote business plan after business plan for small restaurants where the numbers just didn't add up if I wasn't chained to a stove. That meeting with Danny, though it didn't form a partnership, started a friendship, and gave me possibly the greatest insight into myself that years of therapy could have never provided. One single question allowed me to answer several more in the following weeks and months. It helped me mostly define what I didn't want more than what I did, which ultimately led me to feeling OK about opening a restaurant, but only on my terms.

I was now forty-three and had a long way to go towards figuring out what I wanted to do next, but I knew I was moving in the right direction because I was becoming a better version of myself. I was tuned in and searching every day for the answers. I can't say I was 100% sold on opening a restaurant. I can say I knew that if I was going to do it, it would have to go in a certain way. It had to be able to support a chef alongside me. My body was telling me I didn't want to cook all day every day. And, crucially, finally my mind and ego were in a place where I could accept that.

meaty indulgences

I don't eat a lot of meat these days, but when I do, it excites me. Because it's a rarity when I have it, I want it to be rich and messy and delicious. When it comes to the cooking, meat is often a labor of love: slow-cooked braises, long roasts, marinades. It all requires time, patience, care. I like that the recipes in this chapter force my hand and encourage me to slow down, to take my time cooking, and, eventually, savor the fruits of my labor in a long comforting meal that begs to be shared with friends and family. Time, patience, and meals with loved ones are all things that I suddenly gained during my year off from restaurant work, so I equate them with indulgence. Just like enjoying a succulent piece of meat falling from the bone.

"spit roasted" leg of lamb, orange, coriander, honey
pg 181

"spit roasted" leg of lamb, orange, coriander, honey

serves 8–10

The first time I made this dish it was indeed on a spit and it was wonderful to watch the lamb slowly cook until it was deeply charred and caramelized on the outside, yet still pink on the inside. The reality is that most of us don't have spits at our disposal, but luckily, it is easy to replicate the same effects in an oven with results that are just as satisfying. Lamb is by far my favorite meat and it always has been ever since the childhood days when I insisted on ordering whole racks well done. This is a nice dish for when you need to serve a crowd, not just because a leg of lamb is a lot of meat, but also because it's pretty impressive when you present it to your guests.

1 leg of lamb, bone-in
kosher salt

for marinade

zest of 2 oranges, peeled with peeler into large pieces (no pith)
1 head of garlic, peeled and chopped
¼ cup coriander seeds, cracked
2 tablespoons black peppercorns, cracked
½ cup olive oil
¼ cup honey

for roasting

zest of 1 orange, finely chopped
2 heads garlic, broken up with paper skin intact
10 rosemary sprigs

1   Generously salt the leg of lamb and let it sit for at least 1 hour, or, ideally, in the fridge overnight if you have time.
2   Combine all the ingredients for the marinade in a bowl and mix to combine.
3   Rub the marinade all over the lamb.

for roasting

1   Preheat the oven to 425°F.
2   Place the lamb in a large roasting pan. Top with the orange zest, broken garlic heads, and rosemary sprigs.
3   Place the lamb in the oven and cook for 20–25 minutes until it is well browned and caramelized.
4   Turn the oven down to 350°F and cook until rare to medium-rare. Use a thermometer to take the internal temperature at its thickest part, which you want to be at about 115°F for rare, 125°F for medium-rare. Once it reaches temperature, remove it from the oven and let it rest for 10–15 minutes, keeping in mind that the lamb will continue to cook a bit as it rests.
5   Place the lamb on a large cutting board and carve off the bone to serve.

veal and pork meatballs

makes 24–32 meatballs

While I don't make meatballs that often, they create such a fun day of cooking and eating: first you make the sauce, then you form the balls, and then throw in some great crusty bread and sop everything up. I can think of no better way to spend a chilly fall or winter day. And meatballs only get better as leftovers, after they have had more time to soak in the sauce. I have found that using veal and pork makes for not only a flavorful meatball, but also the most tender–two things we all want in a meatball. I like to first roast them in the oven and then finish them by braising in the sauce because the combo gives you a nice outside crust without losing the delicate texture as can happen if you fry or pan sauté them.

three great tricks for keeping the meatballs super moist:
1   Use milk-soaked bread instead of breadcrumbs
2   Lots and lots of olive oil
3   Sautéed onion adds another layer of flavor and moisture

2 cups	day-old bread, torn into small pieces
	milk
½ cup + 3 tablespoons	olive oil, plus more for garnish
1	onion, finely chopped
4	garlic cloves, finely chopped
2 pounds	ground veal
2 pounds	ground pork
½ cup	Pecorino Romano + 2 tablespoons for garnish
½ cup	Parmigiano-Reggiano + 2 tablespoons for garnish
4	eggs
2 tablespoons	fennel seeds
1 tablespoon	garlic powder
1 tablespoon	chili flakes + 1 tablespoon for garnish
¾ tablespoon	kosher salt, plus more to taste
3 quarts	30-clove or Arrabiata sauce (pg 112)
	basil leaves

1   In a large mixing bowl, combine bread with enough milk to cover and allow it to soak until the bread is completely soft.
2   In a medium sauté pan, heat 2 tablespoons olive oil over medium heat and add the onions. Cook until softened, 3–4 minutes, and add the garlic. Cook for another minute or two until the garlic is aromatic, but with no color. Set aside.
3   Mix the veal and pork together by hand in a mixing bowl.
4   To the ground meat add: ½ cup each cheese, the eggs, fennel seeds, garlic powder, 1 tablespoon chili flakes, ½ cup olive oil, and the sautéed onions and garlic. Mix well to combine.
5   Drain the bread from the milk and squeeze out the excess liquid. Add the bread to the seasoned meat mixture and mix well to evenly distribute. Your mixture will be slightly wetter than you are probably used to in a meatball mix. As long as you can form a ball you are good. If you need to make it slightly tighter, add a bit more cheese and/or bread.
6   Season with the salt and mix.

7   Preheat the oven to 450°F.

8   Make a small meat patty and heat a sauté pan to medium-high. Heat 1 tablespoon of olive oil and once it's hot, add the patty. Cook it to test the seasoning. Adjust with more salt if needed. Once the seasoning is correct, form all the meat into balls that are just about ¼ cup (2–2½ ounces) each. They will be bigger than a golf ball, but smaller than a tennis ball. If you can, place the sheet pan in the fridge for an hour so that the meatballs set before cooking. This is optional, but will help them to maintain their shape as they cook.

9   Lay the meatballs on a lightly oiled sheet pan and place them in the oven until they are golden brown on the outside, about 8 minutes. They should not be cooked all the way through.

10 As the meatballs roast, heat the 30-clove or Arrabbiata sauce in a large pot on the stove.

11 Transfer the meatballs to the warm sauce and cook on low heat until they are cooked through, about 10–15 minutes.

12 Remove from the pot and place in bowls. Top with extra sauce and the rest of the grated Pecorino, Parmigiano, olive oil, and chili flakes and garnish with basil leaves.

veal and pork meatballs
pg 182

braised osso buco, fennel soffrito
pg 186

braised osso buco, fennel soffritto

serves 4

This dish has been a staple at my restaurants for a long time, but it was only during my time off that I actually had the time to make it at home for friends and family. This dish is what I turn to first when I'm in the mood for something hearty and warming. As is evident from this book and my restaurant, I have a real fondness for fennel and this dish celebrates it in many forms. The braising liquid and the fennel *soffritto* combine to become the sauce. It is so satisfying and delicious that I never feel like it needs anything else, but feel free to serve this with creamy polenta, braised greens, or even the Chicken Fat Potatoes on page 165.

4	pieces of center cut veal shanks, 2-inches thick, tied with butcher twine
	kosher salt
½ cup	olive oil
3	large bulbs fennel, cut into ¼-inch dice, fronds reserved for plating
2	large carrots, cut into ¼-inch dice
1	large onion, cut into ¼-inch dice
4	garlic cloves, sliced
½ bottle	dry white wine
1 (28-ounce) can	San Marzano tomatoes
1 tablespoon	fennel seeds, ground
½ tablespoon	chili flakes
2	sprigs rosemary
5	sprigs thyme
	fennel pollen

1   Heavily salt the veal shanks on both sides and set aside for at least 1 hour. If you can do this in the fridge overnight, even better.

2   Place a large, heavy-bottomed pot over medium-high heat. Heat ¼ cup olive oil in the pot, and once rippling, add the shanks, searing on all sides until golden brown, about 3–5 minutes per side. Remove from the pan and set aside.

3   Scrape up and discard any burnt pieces (if the pan is too brown, change to a new one). Add the remaining ¼ cup olive oil along with the diced fennel, carrots, and onions to the pot.

4   After 3 minutes, add the sliced garlic. Continue cooking, stirring occasionally, until the *soffritto* is tender and slightly golden, another 5–8 minutes.

5   Return the veal to the pot and add the wine. Cook down until the wine is reduced by half. Transfer the tomatoes to a bowl and crush by hand. Add the tomatoes to the pot along with the ground fennel seeds and chili flakes.

6   Add enough water so that the shanks are covered by almost 1 inch. Cover and turn the heat down to low, cooking on the stovetop until the meat is completely tender and falling off the bone, about 1½–2 hours. (Alternatively, you can place it in a 325°F oven to cook.) In the last 45 minutes of cooking, add the rosemary and thyme. (Adding them late allows the herbs to infuse without overpowering.)

7   Remove the shanks from the pot and turn the heat up to reduce the sauce slightly if is too brothy. You don't want it too thick as it will taste tacky and sticky, but you want it to have a little body.

8   Plate the shanks individually in bowls or all together on a platter. Top with the sauce and sofritto and garnish with lots of fennel pollen and chopped fennel fronds.

mom's brisket (sort of)

serves 10–12

I grew up not really enjoying brisket. But something changed a few years ago and now when I'm home for the holidays I look forward to my mom's brisket, especially the burnt end pieces. I take my cues from hers: she always uses beer and Heinz chili sauce for flavoring, which makes her brisket sweet and tangy. I'm not saying I can do it better (I would never say that!), but the additional aromatics make it a little… enhanced. Thanks for the inspiration, Mom!

1	brisket, whole (10–12-pounds)
	kosher salt
	olive oil
3	onions, sliced into ¼-inch wedges
3 tablespoons	black pepper, coarsely ground
1 tablespoon	chili flakes
1 can	of beer (ale is best)
¾ cup	Heinz chili sauce
1 (14-ounce) can	San Marzano tomatoes, crushed
2	heads of garlic, split in half horizontally
10	sprigs thyme
3	sprigs rosemary

1   Heavily salt the brisket and let it sit for at least an hour. (Overnight in the fridge is best.)

2   Heat a large roasting pan over high heat. Add the olive oil and sear the brisket on both sides until golden, about 5–8 minutes each side. If you do not have a roasting pan large enough to sear on the stove top, heat an oven to 450°F, rub the olive oil on the brisket and place the brisket in the oven for 15–20 minutes until a caramelized crust is formed.

3   Preheat your oven to 350°F. Line the bottom of a clean roasting pan with half of the onions. Place the brisket on top of the onions. Season with the black pepper and chili flakes. Add the beer, chili sauce, tomatoes, the remaining onions, and the garlic and herbs. Cover tightly with foil.

4   Put the roasting pan in the oven and braise until completely cooked through and tender, about 3 hours. (You'll know it's done when you can tear a piece off without too much resistance, but it's not completely falling apart.)

5   Remove from the oven and allow the meat to rest for 30 minutes, then remove it from the pan, reserving the sauce, onions, etc.

6   Slice the brisket and transfer to a platter. Remove the thyme and rosemary sprigs from the sauce before ladling it over the sliced brisket.

pork chop, nectarines, mustard vinaigrette

I was at my neighbor's apartment one night and he challenged me to cook dinner on the fly using only the ingredients he had on hand: a pork chop, some old nectarines, basil, a red onion, and other random pantry items. In less than half an hour we tucked into a juicy grilled pork chop with grilled red onions, nectarines, and mustard vinaigrette, and arugula. Not bad for a completely unplanned pantry cleanout. The lesson here is that sometimes the best meals come from moments of creative fun, when you just let your imagination run wild and ditch the plan. I always use double-cut, very thick pork chops to maximize juiciness, so one chop is enough for two people. And don't believe what they say about cooking pork well done—medium-rare to medium is the sweet spot.

¾ cup	olive oil
1	sprig rosemary, leaves only, chopped
2	garlic cloves, finely chopped
	zest of 1 lemon
2	double-cut pork chops (about 2-inches thick)
	kosher salt
1	red onion, sliced into rings (about ½-inch thick)
¼ cup	whole grain mustard
3 tablespoons	red wine vinegar
3	nectarines, cut into ¼-inch-thick wedges
10	basil leaves
1	bunch arugula

1   Mix 2 tablespoons of the olive oil with the rosemary, garlic, and lemon zest.
2   Rub this marinade all over the pork chops, salt them, and let them sit for 30 minutes.
3   Preheat your grill to medium.
4   Drizzle another tablespoon olive oil on the pork before placing it on the grill. Cook on both sides, continuing to turn for even cooking, until the pork is nicely golden, slightly charred, and cooked to an internal temperature of about 130°F. As these are very thick pieces of pork, it might be hard to gauge the cooking time, so a thermometer is helpful.
5   As the pork chops cook, drizzle 1 tablespoon olive oil on the sliced onions and season with salt. Place the onion slices flat on the grill until charred and wilted. Remove from the grill and set aside.
6   While the pork continues to cook, make the vinaigrette. Whisk together the mustard, red wine vinegar, and ¼ cup olive oil in a bowl and set aside.
7   Once it has reached an internal temperature of about 130°F, remove the pork from the grill and let it rest for 5 minutes before transferring to plates for serving. On top of each chop, arrange the nectarines, followed by the vinaigrette, onions, basil leaves, and arugula. Finish them by drizzling with the remaining ¼ cup olive oil.

steak, spicy red onions, balsamic, arugula   serves 4

These days, I don't eat a lot of steak, but do I enjoy it on those occasions when I do decide to indulge. This is a quick and easy recipe with a great balance of sweet and spicy from Calabrian chili oil and the balsamic vinegar. And it's an example of your not having to break the bank to enjoy great meat: While a dry aged strip is obviously awesome, I often prefer the lesser steak cuts like hanger and skirt because they are tender and full of flavor. Since you save a little by using a hanger, you can splurge on the olive oil and balsamic you use for finishing because, along with the spicy onions, they are the heroes of this dish.

24-ounce	hanger steak, or whatever cut you prefer, cut into four 6-ounce pieces
	kosher salt
	black pepper
6 tablespoons	olive oil
2	red onions, sliced into ½-inch-thick rings
3 tablespoons	red wine vinegar
	zest of half an orange
1 tablespoon	Calabrian chili oil (from a jar of Calabrian chiles)
1 cup	arugula
	coarse sea salt, for finishing
	extra good-quality olive oil, for finishing
	aged balsamic vinegar

1   Season the steak on both sides with salt and pepper.
2   Place a large cast-iron pan over high heat. Pour 3 tablespoons olive oil into the pan and once the oil is heated and rippling, add the steaks. Sear until medium-rare, golden and nicely crusted, about 5–7 minutes on each side. Remove from the pan and set aside to rest.
3   While the steak cooks, heat another large pan to medium and add the remaining 3 tablespoons of olive oil. Season the onion slices with salt and pepper and place them in one even layer in the hot pan and sear until golden and tender, about 3–4 minutes.
4   Deglaze the pan with the red wine vinegar and add the orange zest. Cook the onions until they are just tender and don't become too wilted or soft. Add the chili oil, mix to evenly distribute, and turn off the heat.
5   Allow the steaks to rest before slicing and transferring to a serving platter. Top with the onions and arugula and season with the coarse sea salt. Drizzle with olive oil and balsamic.

short ribs with walnut gremolata

serves 4

I got to cook for my dad's birthday at home during my year off. I told him to pick up some short ribs, so I knew that would be the star of whatever I was going to make. But everything else was up in the air because I never know what the hell is in their house. When I got there I rifled through their pantry and used what I could find. I came up with this dish. For most people, just making braised short ribs would be enough of a challenge, but not for this over-achieving chef. I felt it needed texture and another flavor component. Introducing anchovies to a sauce adds a touch of salt, and dare I say one of the most overused words, umami, while the walnut-orange combo brings the texture and an additional flavor dimension. Serve over farro or any other nutty grain to really take this dish to the next level.

3 pounds	of beef short ribs, cut into 2-inch lengths
1½ tablespoons	kosher salt
2 teaspoons	ground coriander
3 teaspoons	smoked paprika
5 tablespoons	olive oil
2	medium-large carrots, peeled and cut into ¼-inch dice
1½	Spanish onions, peeled and cut into ¼-inch dice
5	celery stalks, cut into ¼-inch dice
10	garlic cloves, peeled and sliced thick
1½ cups	red wine
2 cups	chicken stock (if you don't have chicken stock you can use water; the cooking of the vegetables and short ribs will still garner incredible flavor)
1	fresh bay leaf
8	sprigs thyme
¼	bunch Italian flat-leaf parsley
7 ounces	San Marzano tomatoes, crushed by hand (I use half of a 14-ounce can)
½ teaspoon	chili flakes
2	anchovies in oil, drained and broken into small pieces
2	strips orange zest

1   Place the short ribs on a tray or large plate and season evenly on all sides with the salt, coriander, and 2 teaspoons of the smoked paprika. Let them sit for a minimum of 1 hour. If you have time, it is even better to let the meat cure overnight, covered in the refrigerator.
2   Preheat the oven to 325°F.
3   Heat a large heavy-bottomed pot over medium heat. Add 3 tablespoons olive oil followed by the short ribs. Sear on all sides for about 3 minutes per side to achieve a nice golden crust, while also rendering some of the fat. Use tongs to remove the short ribs from the pan and set aside.
4   Lower the heat to medium-low and add the remaining 2 tablespoons olive oil to the rendered beef fat before adding the *soffritto* (carrots, onions, and celery). Sweat the vegetables while stirring occasionally for about 3–5 minutes, then add the garlic. Continue to sauté for another 5 minutes or until tender and the onions are translucent, but not caramelized.
5   Add the short ribs back to the pot, followed by the red wine. Let the wine reduce by half before adding the stock (or water), herbs, tomatoes, chili flakes, anchovy, orange zest, and remaining paprika. Cover and place the pot in the oven.
6   Cook for approximately 2½ hours or until the meat is tender and falling off the bone.

for the walnut gremolata

¼ **cup**	finely chopped walnuts
	zest of 1 orange, finely grated
¾ **cup**	parsley leaves, dried on a paper towel and finely chopped
1	clove garlic, peeled and finely minced

Combine all the ingredients in a bowl and mix well.

for the finish

	short ribs
	cooking liquid, with vegetables still in it
2 tablespoons	prepared walnut gremolata
	celery leaves

1   Place one or two short ribs in each of four bowls. Cover each portion with about ½ cup of the sauce, making sure to include some of the vegetables as well.
2   Garnish with the gremolata and celery leaves.

reemerging

May 3, 2014 was approaching quickly. That day would mark exactly one year since I had left the workforce. My year off was nearly over and I still didn't have a solid plan. How could that be? As my bank account balance dipped lower and lower, my anxiety levels got higher and higher.

Just about the only thing I knew was that I needed to go back to work, but I had not figured out what that would or should look like. I was pretty close to signing a deal with a wealthy restaurateur in a space that had nothing special going for it in a location I didn't particularly love. It was the most immediate, sensible solution to get me back to work, but it didn't feel right. I knew these were not the right partners for me and I also knew it was not the long-term solution I was seeking. My gut was speaking to me—make that shouting—and it was telling me to keep looking. But without the luxury of money or time I felt an uneasy pressure that weighed on me greatly. Opportunities with people like Danny Meyer, the famed founder of Union Square Hospitality Group who I so desperately wanted to partner with, didn't pan out, and the people who wanted me, I wasn't interested in. A combination of snobbishness and stubbornness made me feel like I couldn't apply for any job, and as a high-profile chef, I didn't want a job as a line cook or barista. In spite of the mounting pressure, I remained hopeful that I would find the right thing. I didn't want my time off to culminate with a dead-end job. To stop hemorrhaging money and buy myself more time, I toned down on the lunching, shopping, and going out for dinner.

Being at home more often had some drawbacks, but one of the fortunate consequences was that I became quite close with my upstairs neighbors, Sean and Maria. Sean, specifically, had a keen interest in the restaurant business and food. (He is actually an excellent cook.) We would talk about restaurants and the meetings I was having. He always had a skeptical look in his eye, twirling his hair, lost in thought as I spoke. His mind never rests. Finally, he told me to stop talking to all these other people and partner with him. I immediately said no. He was a finance guy whose only restaurant experience was some financial consulting he did for a local restaurant group in the West Village. I needed to go back to work ASAP, and I knew partnering with him would delay that.

Sean is aggressive and persistent in the best possible way, so despite my turning him down, I found myself in conversations about our partnership and what that would look like: our roles, the finances, what kind of company we each envisioned. As time passed and discussions continued, I became more and more intrigued. But none of this solved the issue of my current state of financial affairs. Sean suggested I get a consulting gig, as if finding a job like that were as easy as picking up the phone.

But, as fate would have it, a few days later I got a call from a friend in need of a chef. While I explained that I could not be her permanent chef, I offered up the idea of consulting short term. She was opening a new location of her wine bar and needed to get it up and running. Our philosophies on what the food should look like aligned—the menu would be a less Italian version of the *cicchetti* bars I had become obsessed with on my recent trip to Venice. So, I made a deal I felt very comfortable with that would support me for the next six months (hopefully), and get me back into a kitchen, for better or worse. I quickly set out to develop the menu in a kitchen that was even smaller than the one in my apartment, which I didn't even think could be possible in a professional space. It had two induction burners, a small fryer, and two tiny convection ovens that were basically fancy toaster ovens. I eagerly created an extremely ambitious menu (in hindsight probably too ambitious for this little place) but to this day it is up there with my favorite food I have ever cooked, much of it inspired by the trip to Italy.

Initially, consulting was cool. It was freeing. Even though I was doing an opening, it wasn't all on me. I could come and go as I pleased. It didn't interrupt my Pilates dates. I would hire a staff, train a staff, leave them recipes and move on to the next thing.

Easy! Turns out, not so much. Staff was impossible to find so I ended up cooking like an entry-level cook in this tiny kitchen day in and day out for months. I was a prep cook. I showed up at 8:00 a.m. every morning and left at 11:00 p.m. every evening. I was somehow right back where I started. How the hell did this happen? I was fairly miserable. I loved the planning and developing, but my intention was never to actually work the "line," if you could even call it that. On top of that, the feeling of giving all of myself to something, all this great food and creativity, to just walk away and not really "own" it started to feel bad. I had always been so attached to the places I worked. It was the only way I knew how to do it. Give everything. Act like it's yours. Except this time, it wasn't. I was walking away in five or less months. It wouldn't be long before I would have nothing to do with it and that was tough to get past.

Toward the end of those six months, I picked up more consulting gigs. Nothing that I'm proud of or care to share much about. They were mostly comprised of fixing bad concepts and teaching people who had no knowledge of Italian food how to cook it. I made a ton of money doing it, which was the goal, but I wasn't excited about it. I felt completely uninspired, but I had bills to pay. In spite of the lack of inspiration, at one point I thought I wanted to start a consulting company in part because the money was great, but also because I loved, in theory, the excitement of moving from project to project without being tied down. But, that idea passed when I quickly learned that I love stability more. I was not cut out for the constant hustle. The staffing epidemic in New York that saw me thrown into fourteen-hour days, and the monotony of day-to-day operations also made me unsure that I even wanted a restaurant. It scared the shit out of me. I liked the idea of a restaurant, but wasn't so sure I liked the reality of it anymore.

In my off time, I was still mulling over the partnership idea with Sean. Nothing was set in stone, but we definitely were on the path to joining forces. I knew we shared business values and really that's what cinched it for me. At the time, I didn't even fully understand how smart he is, and how driven. I just knew he really wanted this to happen, in part because he wanted to help me have a restaurant, but also because he wanted something new and different for himself. As residents of the West Village, we were at first determined to find a space in the neighborhood we called home. But, over the course of my time off, I had easily looked at more than twenty spaces and it had proved frustrating. They were too expensive or had major structural issues. It was defeating.

Toward the end of my tenure at my grand consulting job, Sean texted that he wanted to introduce me to people with a space in Williamsburg that we could potentially be part of. My first reaction was—and this is a direct quote—"I am not fucking opening in Williamsburg." I was naïve. I didn't know Williamsburg. I thought of it as the place that my twenty-five-year-old, hipster, tattooed cooks lived. I went to look to appease my soon-to-be partner. The space was a grungy auto body shop on a nondescript corner on the north side of the neighborhood. I had no idea where I was. With a good eye and a ton of vision, the building had potential. Although I had both, I was still not sold on opening a restaurant in Brooklyn. I was not a Brooklyn girl. I was a Manhattanite. Except for five years in Chicago, I had lived and worked in Manhattan my whole adult life. I worked all these years to open my first restaurant in Brooklyn? NO! That was August 2014.

Time went on and Sean and I, looking like tourists, would walk around Williamsburg, exploring, people watching, and wondering, *what if*? We deliberated, we continued looking at spaces across the river, but something about this little corner kept drawing us back. I was still lost, not just in Williamsburg, but still on the fence about the challenges of owning a restaurant. But I needed to make a move. I needed to stop worrying about the next fifteen years. I told myself that nothing is forever and that if I went for it in Williamsburg and then hated it, I could figure out a way to get out of it.

In November 2014, we decided to move ahead. We were opening a restaurant. In Brooklyn. Though many people were surprised at my decision, no one as much as I.

fish

True to my childhood identity as a picky eater, fish was not at the top of my willing-to-eat list. The only kinds I could get down were heaping piles of something fried, like smelts, or a mild, white fish, like sole, drowning in so much butter that it could have been anything. The redeeming quality of both overpowering (and full of delicious fat) preparations was that I didn't really know I was eating fish. As I've developed as a chef, however, my tastes in the fish department have changed quite a bit, and you need only glance at my restaurant menus at Lilia to see that I have a deep appreciation for all things fish and seafood. I've found that fish provides the best canvas to express both mild and bold flavors, while also lending itself to a variety of cooking methods from steaming to poaching to grilling to roasting. As I've changed my diet and adapted to healthier eating, fish, along with vegetables, has become a centerpiece of my meals. Ironic that the two food groups I detested most as a child are what I can't live without today. I had no idea what I was missing out on!

salt roasted fish, olives, capers

serves 4

Cracking open a hardened baked salt crust to discover the fragrant, tender, steaming fish enclosed inside is one of the most satisfying feelings a cook can have. Don't be intimidated by the copious amount of salt in this recipe; while it does season the fish it is not overwhelming. The salt simply serves as a cooking vessel and allows the fish to steam, while absorbing all the aromatics. It does take some trial and error as you can't see the fish until it is done, but you will get used to your oven and proper cooking times. A good rule of thumb is about 10–12 minutes per pound, depending on your oven. It's better to undercook the fish a tiny bit and have to flash it in the oven than overcook it and have it be a mushy mess that you can't recover. While this dish is somewhat labor-intensive, the impressive and flavorful result is worth every moment.

for the olive vinaigrette

½ cup	pitted Taggiasca olives, smashed
¼ cup	capers
2	garlic cloves, thinly sliced and lightly sautéed
	zest of 1 orange
	zest of 1 lemon
¼ cup	red wine vinegar
1 teaspoon	chili flakes
½ cup	olive oil

Stir all the ingredients together in a mixing bowl and set aside, allowing the flavors to meld until the fish is ready.

for the fish

1 box	Diamond kosher salt
¼ cup	coriander seeds
¼ cup	fennel seeds
1 tablespoon	chili flakes
1	whole fish, such as branzino or sea bream (2–3 pounds)
5	sprigs thyme
5	sprigs marjoram
1	sprig rosemary
3	slices of lemon, cut ¼-inch thick
3	garlic cloves, peeled

1   Preheat the oven to 450°F.
2   Mix the salt, coriander, fennel seeds, and chili flakes together in a large bowl. Gradually add water until you have a consistency similar to wet sand and set aside.
3   Fill the cavity of the fish with the herbs, lemon, and garlic.
4   Line a half sheet pan with a piece of parchment paper and place a third of the seasoned salt mixture in a mound on the bottom of the tray. Use your hands to shape it into an oval that is slightly larger than the fish. Place the fish on top of the mound of salt.
5   Top the fish with enough of the remaining wet salt mixture to cover it and use your hands to shape the salt into an oval completely surrounding the fish.
6   Place the fish in the oven and cook for 20 to 30 minutes, depending on the weight of your fish. The crust should be completely hard when coming out of the oven.
7   Gently crack the salt shell by tapping it with the side of a spoon. Use your hands to gently remove the shell from the fish.
8   Carefully transfer the entire fish from the cooking tray to a serving platter using a large spatula and spoon to hold each end.
9   Top the fish with the olive vinaigrette. You may have some left over, which is great because it will last in the fridge and is perfect for topping grilled chicken or fish.
10 Gently remove the flesh of the fish from the bone to eat.

salt roasted fish, olives, capers
pg 196

tuna, parsley, and chive salsa verde
pg 200

tuna, parsley, and chive salsa verde

serves 4

The star of this dish is the herbaceous salsa verde, my favorite condiment of them all. While it is a little labor intensive because there are more ingredients than most of my recipes and everything needs to be cut by hand, I assure you the payoff is worth it because it has the power to instantly transform and brighten whatever you choose to put it on. Whether it's humble boiled potatoes or a delicate piece of tuna, you will want to sop up every last drop of sauce.

for the salsa verde

1 cup	chopped parsley
½ cup	chopped chives
¼ cup	minced tarragon
6	anchovy fillets, finely chopped
2	garlic cloves, finely chopped
1	large or 2 small shallots, finely diced
1 cup	olive oil
3	eggs
1½ tablespoons	Dijon mustard
1½ tablespoons	red wine vinegar, plus more to taste

1   Mix the parsley, chives, tarragon, anchovy, garlic, and shallots together in a small bowl. Cover with the olive oil. Set aside until ready to use.
2   Place the eggs in a small pot, cover with cold water, and bring to a simmer. Remove from heat and let sit exactly 4 minutes. Remove the eggs from the water and transfer to an ice bath to stop the cooking. Once cooled, peel them and add only the yolks to the bowl of herbs along with the mustard. Mix together until blended—the consistency will be slightly textured, not smooth.
3   Once you're ready to cook and serve the fish, transfer ¾ cup of the herb base to a small bowl and whisk in the vinegar. Taste and add more vinegar if necessary— the sauce should have a bright acidic bite to it. Set aside until tuna is cooked.

for the tuna and finish

4	6-ounce tuna fillets (1 ½-inches thick)
	kosher salt
3 tablespoons	olive oil
	salsa verde (above)

1   Preheat your grill to high.
2   Drizzle the olive oil on the fish and season with salt.
3   Place the fish on the grill and cook until rare to medium-rare, 2–3 minutes on each side.
4   Transfer to plates and smother with the prepared salsa verde.

turbot, lemon, truffles

serves 4

There are times when it's truly great to be a chef, and one of them is when you have friends in the industry who spontaneously gift you luxury items, like truffles. Usually if I have truffles around I make pasta, but one time something got me excited to go a different direction and I chose to match with bright lemon and sweet turbot, which is my hands-down favorite fish. Both black and white truffles will work for this dish, and if you can't get your hands on fresh ones, or just want to save your budget for something else, there are many decent jarred and canned truffle products on the market that you can use. Whatever you do, just don't use truffle oil because it will never taste the same as a true truffle.

4 6-ounce turbot fillets
1 teaspoon kosher salt
4 tablespoons olive oil, plus 2 tablespoons for finishing
juice and zest of 1 lemon, plus another ½ lemon for finishing
truffles (as many as you can get your hands on)

1   Preheat the oven to 400°F.
2   Season one side of the fish with the salt. (Turbot is a very thin fish, so I only season one side.) Place the fillets in one even layer in a baking dish.
3   Drizzle 4 tablespoons olive oil all over the fish and top it with the lemon zest. Drizzle the lemon juice over the top and place the baking dish in the oven to cook until the fish is opaque and just cooked through, 8–10 minutes.
4   Once cooked, remove the fish from the oven and transfer each fillet to a plate, along with some of the pan juices. Finish each with a bit of the remaining olive oil and a squeeze of lemon juice before generously shaving truffles all over the top.

turbot, lemon, truffles
pg 201

ceviche style bass
pg 204

ceviche style bass

This is a great warm-weather lunch or appetizer to start a light dinner because it is fresh, clean, and full of vibrant flavors from the lime, spice, and herbs. Because this is ceviche-style and the only "cooking" that happens is courtesy of an acid bath, it is extra important that you buy the freshest possible fish from the market. So, if bass is unavailable or not the freshest option, any white fleshed, mild fish will work–just as long as it's fresh!

8 ounces	bass (black or branzino work great), skin off
	juice of 3 limes, plus the finely grated zest of 1
1 tablespoon	olive oil
	sea salt
6–8	basil leaves, smaller ones
1	Fresno pepper, sliced into thin rings

1   Slice the fillets of bass into very thin strips, approximately 2 inches long and ⅛-inch thick.
2   Arrange the strips in one layer on a plate and juice the limes over the top so that it is evenly distributed over all the fish. Let the fish sit in the juice to effectively "cook" until the flesh becomes opaque, approximately 10–12 minutes.
3   Once the fish is finished marinating in the juice, season with the olive oil, sea salt, and lime zest. Garnish with the basil leaves and Fresno peppers.

fish stew, marjoram, citrus, chiles

serves 4–6

This dish is my go-to for a healthy, quick, and super flavorful meal. Once all the prep is complete, it takes only twelve minutes or so to make and is bursting with flavor. The fish is all cooked in my spicy Arrabbiata sauce (page 112) and brightened with marjoram and citrus zest. You could add beans or chickpeas to make it heartier, but, honestly, I think it's just perfect as it is. The only thing it's lacking is a vehicle to sop up all the sauce—easily fixed with a crusty loaf of toasted country bread.

2 tablespoons	olive oil, plus 1 tablespoon for finishing
5	garlic cloves, thinly sliced
2 cups	Arrabbiata sauce (page 112)
2 dozen	littleneck clams, scrubbed
1 dozen	PEI mussels, washed and de-bearded
1½ pounds	bass or other mild, white fish (cod, snapper, etc.) cut into 2½ ounce pieces
	zest of 1 orange, julienned into 1-inch lengths, plus juice from half the fruit
	kosher salt
1 teaspoon	chili flakes
2	sprigs marjoram, leaves only

1   Place a wide pan over low heat and add 2 tablespoons olive oil, along with the sliced garlic. Sweat until aromatic, but without color, about 2 minutes.
2   Add the Arrabbiata sauce. This dish is meant to be like a stew, so the sauce shouldn't be overly thick. You'll likely have to add ½ cup to 1 cup water to loosen the sauce.
3   Add both the clams and mussels to the sauce and cover. Cook for about 5 minutes, checking under the lid once or twice to remove each clam and mussel from the pan just as it opens so they don't overcook. Transfer the cooked shellfish to a bowl and set aside.
4   Season the bass with salt and add it to the pan. Simmer for about 3–5 minutes. Once the bass is cooked through, return the mussels and clams back to the pan, along with the orange juice and half of the zest. Mix to combine flavors. Taste and add salt if needed.
5   Transfer equal portions of the stew to individual bowls or all of it onto a large serving platter (more fun to put in the center of the table). Garnish with the remaining orange zest, chili flakes, and marjoram. Drizzle with the remaining 1 tablespoon olive oil.

grilled swordfish, hot and sweet peppers

serves 4

There are so many varieties of peppers available at markets in the summer that it can be hard to choose, but the good news with this dish is that you don't have to! Buy an assortment of different shapes, colors, and sizes—you can even throw a few fresh hot chiles into the oven, too. Although the peppers act as a sauce and garnish to the swordfish, they are a standout in their own right and equally delicious as a side dish, or served with toasted bread.

for the marinated peppers

1½ pounds	assorted sweet peppers
¼ cup + 3 tablespoons	olive oil
½ teaspoon	kosher salt
3 tablespoons	Calabrian chiles in their oil, more if you like things very spicy
4 tablespoons	capers
3	garlic cloves, cut into thick slices
¼ cup	red wine vinegar

1   Preheat the oven to 400°F.
2   Toss the fresh peppers in 3 tablespoons of olive oil and the salt.
3   Scatter them in one even layer on a sheet pan and place it into the oven. Roast for approximately 15 minutes, or until the skin is blistering and the flesh is tender. You are not looking for color.
4   Remove the peppers from the oven, transfer them to a bowl, and cover with plastic wrap. Let them steam for 10 minutes to make the skin easier to remove.
5   Once they are cool enough to handle, peel away the skin and remove the stems and seeds from the peppers. Transfer the cleaned peppers to a bowl and add the Calabrian chiles, capers, remaining ¼ cup of olive oil, garlic, and vinegar. Allow the peppers to marinate for at least 15 minutes, but the longer the better.

for the swordfish

4	6-ounce fillets of swordfish (1½-inches thick)
3 tablespoons	olive oil
	kosher salt
	marinated peppers (above)
2	sprigs mint, leaves only

1   Heat the grill to high.
2   Rub the olive oil on the fish, season with salt, and place it on the hot grill. Cook for 3–4 minutes on each side, until medium-rare or medium. Do not cook the swordfish to well-done as it will dry out.
3   Remove the cooked fish from the grill and transfer to plates or a large serving platter. Top with the marinated peppers and garnish with the mint.

calabrian chili grilled lobster serves 4

I first made this lobster at a lovely summer party and watched everyone flock to it like vultures. The lobsters came right off the grill, went straight into this citrusy spicy vinaigrette, then disappeared. And it's such a fun messy dish to dig into. While I think the overt heat is definitely the best part of this dish, the citrus offers some balance and respite, so if you like things a little less spicy just tone it down by adding more. And this zesty Calabrian vinaigrette does not have to be reserved only for lobster, it also makes a great sauce for other fish and vegetable dishes. You can steam or boil the lobsters if you don't have a grill, but you might miss out on the extra flavor of the smoke and char. No matter how you cook the lobsters, just be careful not to overcook them because no amount of delicious sauce can save rubbery, dry lobster meat!

1½ cups	Calabrian chili paste
2	garlic cloves, chopped and lightly sautéed in 1 tablespoon olive oil
	juice and zest of 1 lemon
	zest of 1 orange
	juice of 2 oranges
6 tablespoons	olive oil
4	1½-pound lobsters

1 Separate the chiles from their oil over a bowl, using a fine mesh strainer and reserving the oil. Finely chop the chiles and transfer both the chopped chiles along with 2 tablespoons of the reserved oil to a large mixing bowl.

2 Add the garlic, lemon, and orange zests, and 4 tablespoons olive oil to the bowl. Mix to combine and set aside. To preserve the vibrant flavor of the citrus juice and let it have maximum impact in the sauce, add the lemon and orange juices just before you grill the lobster. Stir to combine.

3 Preheat your grill to high.

4 Break off the claws and tail from each lobster. Split the tails in half lengthwise, leaving the meat in the shell, and drizzle the meat with the remaining 2 tablespoons olive oil. With the back of a heavy chef's knife, slightly crack the claws.

5 Place the claws on the grill first and cook for approximately 3 minutes, before adding the tails, flesh side down. Cook them together for another 5 minutes or so, occasionally turning the claws as they cook. In the final minute of cooking, turn the tails over to briefly cook on the shell side.

6 Transfer the tails directly into the bowl with the vinaigrette. Before adding the claws to the vinaigrette, widen the cracks in the shell a bit more to make it slightly easier to remove the flesh while you eat. Toss the lobster in the vinaigrette so that it is well coated and dig in!

grilled swordfish, hot and sweet peppers
pg 206

calabrian chili grilled lobster
pg 207

grilled clams, butter, lemon, herbed garlic bread
pg 211

grilled clams, butter, lemon, herbed garlic bread

serves 4–6

Nothing screams summer more than throwing a bunch of clams on the grill, tossing them with butter, and opening a bottle of rosé. The herb butter in this recipe is an exciting but simple addition, and it yields more than you will need for this dish. Wrap it up and save it in your fridge to quickly brighten up fish, meat, chicken, vegetables, or even pasta.

herb butter

1 cup	parsley leaves
½ cup	roughly chopped chives
1 pound	butter, room temperature
1 tablespoon	chopped garlic
	kosher salt

1   Fill a pot with about 4 quarts of heavily salted water and bring it to a boil. Once boiling, blanch the herbs for 15–20 seconds in the water. Transfer the blanched herbs to an ice bath to stop the cooking.
2   Once cold, remove the herbs, squeeze them to get rid of excess water, and place them in a blender, pureeing until smooth. You may have to add a touch of water to get the puree moving.
3   Transfer the herb puree to a large mixing bowl along with the room temperature butter and garlic and mix well. Season with salt. The butter should be bright green. Set aside until you are ready to use.

for the clams

4 dozen	Littleneck clams
¾ pound	butter
4	garlic cloves, finely minced
	juice of 2 lemons
	zest of 1 lemon
½	loaf country style bread, cut into 1-inch-thick slices

1   Place the clams in a large mixing bowl or pot under cold running water until there is no trace of sand.
2   Melt the butter in a saucepan over low heat and add the garlic. Gently cook the garlic until just aromatic with no color, 2 minutes. Add the lemon juice and zest to the pan and remove from the heat. Set aside as you cook the clams.
3   Place the clams on a very hot preheated grill and close the lid. Check the clams every minute or so and as they start to open, remove them one by one and transfer them to a large bowl on the side. Pour half of the melted lemon-garlic butter over them and toss. Reserve the rest of the butter for extra dipping.
4   As the clams cook, place the bread on the grill and cook for 1–2 minutes until the slices are nicely toasted, but not too charred. When you're ready to serve, generously spread the herb butter on the bread and serve alongside the clams.

the aftermath

Lilia opened its doors on January 19, 2016, the culmination of what was supposed to be only a year off, but that had essentially turned into almost two and a half years. It took sixteen months to decide on something to do, and another fourteen months to build it. It's true that after the initial year, I had consulting gigs and was working on this restaurant project, but I wasn't fully immersed back into the restaurant game until Lilia opened. The best part was that I finally had a complete life. And, it was a life that I liked. I was healthy, and while I was very nervous in the build-up to Lilia, I was excited at the same time.

I was also in what I believed was a healthy relationship. It was not without its challenges, but I thought I could count on us. I attributed the bumpy road to our concurrent hectic work lives and thought once everything was settled and Lilia opened, we would come out of it. But I was wrong. Two weeks into opening, my girlfriend left me. At first I hoped it would be temporary, but in the end that wasn't the case. I had been so close to the stability I longed for: a steady personal life, good mental and physical health, and a restaurant of my own where I could make sure that I didn't have to work the fourteen-hour days that I no longer had the stamina or drive for. I looked forward to working productively and efficiently so I could keep the room for the other things in my life. I wanted to make sure there was time for a relationship, Pilates, my friends, and family. I was excited to do things differently and wanted to prove that you don't have to have a terrible life to own a restaurant. I wanted to prove that to be a good leader, you actually had to separate yourself from the day-to-day every so often. Suddenly, I was alone with a restaurant. My biggest nightmare. My sense of balance, and my heart, were shattered.

I stood at the pass every night for those first four months, performing. My stage had been built, literally, in my very open and exposed kitchen. There was no hiding in the basement or behind a swinging door. I was there, exposed and raw and feeling like shit. But at 5:30 every evening, the show began. And I stood there smiling and saying *thank you* for all the gracious accolades and compliments. I was grateful for the busy moments that allowed me to get lost in work and grant me a temporary interlude from the internal strife. I was good at faking it, which I did to make sure my personal tumult made no negative impact on the success of the restaurant that I had worked so hard to build. I was moving tickets and plating giant lamb steaks. I was back leading a team and making sure they were happy. Ironically, I had rekindled the love for my career, but had lost the love in my personal life. It made me really question whether the idea of balance that I so desperately sought was even possible.

Opening my own place was supposed to be the happiest moment of my life. I had this gorgeous restaurant that I curated every aspect of, from the food, to the uniforms, to the dishes, to the branding. I had an amazing business partner that was there for me every step of the way. I had people from all stages of my life so excited that I had finally achieved my dream of opening a restaurant. In the end, I never had the epiphany I was hoping to have that would make me try something else, so I did the thing I knew how to do, but on my own terms. I knew how to open a restaurant and I knew how to cook. And my cooking was better than it had ever been. I had stripped away the bullshit. I didn't care about stars or reviews except to acknowledge that favorable ones were good for business. I was just cooking the food that was important to me. The food that I wanted to eat, the food that I cooked in my tiny home kitchen. I was excited to cook food that I hoped the public would crave.

As time passed and I grew into Lilia, I came to adore it. I have become the best version of myself that I have ever been, especially inside the kitchen. I wasn't conscious of the growth my time off had allowed until my mental strength was put to the test in the stress of opening my own restaurant in the midst of navigating personal turbulence. And I've continued to be mellow, and don't get upset by all the little things that used to drive me crazy. I believe in what I am doing. I love being there, even when there are long days. The goal had always been to create my ideal version of a neighborhood restaurant that I would want to eat in every day, and even more importantly, create the restaurant that I would be thrilled to work in every day. I wanted my team to feel the same way. I am happy to say that not only do I believe those things are true, but also frequently noted by guests peering into our open kitchen.

Since my time off, I have been able to set boundaries so that I can live the life I want. I take days off. If I want to go to dinner, I make it so that I can. My staff respects my privacy and they are responsible enough to make the kitchen run smoothly even in my absence. My shoulder doesn't hurt from hunching over constant knife work because I choose to not do very much of it. My open kitchen allows me to talk to guests all night long, something that I cherish, and now my smiles are real. We designed the layout in such a way that I am part of both the kitchen and the dining room action and it's perfect. I hope never to be stuck behind another closed door kitchen. If I head out of town for an event, I am eager to get back to work. Over the past twenty-three years, I have liked a lot of my jobs, but I've certainly never *missed* them. Then again, Lilia isn't a job, it's a restaurant I helped to create. I imagine it's similar to having a child: I want to see it develop and thrive. I don't want to miss a moment of its growth. I take the good with the bad and it gives me a greater sense of purpose. These are feelings I never thought I would have in my career.

Not to mention that I am completely thrilled to have navigated a restaurant opening and other challenges without gaining any of my weight back. I can officially say that I am no longer an emotional eater. If this was three years ago, I would most likely be back at 198. I would have eaten every emotion, both good and bad, along with spoonfuls of Häagen-Dazs. Luckily, I have never been a big drinker, but boy were the moments I wish I was so I could escape. Instead, I now handle my stress through exercise and long moments of personal introspection. And, a lot of tearful phone calls to friends and family, who have been beyond supportive.

Lilia, the place that it has become and the place that it will grow into, could never have happened if I didn't take my crazy leap into the unknown world of unemployment. In strictly financial terms, it's not a wise decision, but in spite of the hard times, and the bottomed out bank account, it was the best possible thing I have ever done for myself. I had some of the greatest experiences of my life. I am a better chef because of that time, a better leader, and, without a doubt, a better person.

And the biggest surprise of all? I now not only own a restaurant in Brooklyn, but I am a full-time resident! When the lease on my West Village apartment ended eight months after Lilia opened, I did what made the most sense: I moved across the bridge to be closer to the restaurant. I could walk to work, I could pop in to say hi, or surprise guests on a whim. I exchanged my charming West Village apartment complete with fireplace and terrible kitchen, for a brand-new home boasting a dishwasher, washer and dryer, marble countertops, and space to actually roll out pasta dough at home.

Finally, at forty-five, with a restaurant to call my own and my first adult apartment, I feel grown up—which might have been what I was seeking all along.

after dinner

I am not cut out for baking. I am impatient. I don't like waiting for results. I don't particularly like measuring. Baking is messy. Sugar is sticky. Let's just say I do not have a future as a pastry chef. While I might not be a master at making desserts, I do, however, enjoy a touch of sweet to end a meal. This chapter is all about great endings and easy preparations. And I even threw in one cake, just to challenge myself.

olive oil cake, candied citrus, whipped cream

serves 8

Olive oil cake is a very humble dessert that I always wanted as part of my repertoire and now it finally is. We serve it at Lilia and people always ask me for this recipe, so I had to include it here. I like to change the fruits with the season, favoring citrus in the winter, cherries in the late spring and early summer, and stone fruits in the later summer. Though, frankly, my favorite part is the fluffy cloud of whipped cream draping over the top.

for the cake

2 cups + 2 tablespoons	all purpose flour
1¾ cups	sugar
½ teaspoon	baking powder
½ teaspoon	baking soda
1 cup + 2 tablespoons	olive oil, plus more for the pan
1¼ cup	milk
¼ cup	orange juice
3	eggs
	zest of 2 oranges
	zest of 1 lemon

1 Preheat the oven to 350°F.
2 In a bowl, whisk together the flour, sugar, baking powder, and baking soda.
3 In a separate bowl, whisk together the olive oil, milk, orange juice, eggs, and citrus zests.
4 Gradually add the wet ingredients to the dry ingredients while stirring to combine. Whisk until the batter is smooth.
5 Lightly oil the inside rim of a 9-inch springform pan with a bit of olive oil. Line the bottom of the pan with a circle of parchment paper.
6 Pour the batter into the baking pan, using a rubber spatula to scrape all of it out and make sure it is in one even layer. Place in the oven and bake for 1 hour. Check the center with a knife, it should come out clean when the cake is done.

for the citrus

1	orange, sliced into paper thin rings
2½ cups	sugar
1 cup	water

1 Place the orange slices in a pot and cover with cold water. Bring to a boil. Drain. Repeat 3 times. This will remove any bitterness.
2 Place the sugar and water in a small saucepan. Slowly heat to dissolve the sugar. Add the oranges and cook until just tender and sweet, about 10–15 minutes on low heat.

whipped cream

1 cup   heavy cream
1 tablespoon   sugar

Combine the cream and sugar in a bowl and whisk to soft peaks.

To Serve

Slice the cake into wedges and top each with a giant dollop of whipped cream. Garnish with some of the candied citrus.

lemon granita with whipped cream

serves 4

Like many kids, I grew up eating Marino's Italian Ices, those little yellow cups scrawled with green writing that came with a wooden "spoon," whose woody flavor I often thought tasted more flavorful than the ice itself. I don't know if the people at Marino's were inspired by it, but *granita* is the shaved ice of Italy, popular in places like Sicily and the Amalfi Coast. While nothing compares to the *granita* made with the ripened, sun-kissed lemons of coastal Italy, this recipe makes a version that's damn close. If you want to relive some of your creamsicle days, add a little whipped cream, vanilla ice cream, or gelato. It's also perfect on its own, a light and refreshing way to end a meal. While lemon is my favorite, *granita* can be made with any fruit, and even coffee.

2¼ cups   sugar
4½ cups   water
3 cups   lemon juice
          zest of 3 lemons
          pinch of kosher salt

1   Make the simple syrup by combining the sugar and 2¼ cups water in a small saucepan over low heat. Gently warm until sugar is dissolved. Remove from the heat and cool the syrup.
2   Once cool, transfer the syrup to a large mixing bowl along with the remaining 2¼ cups water and other remaining ingredients. Stir to combine and transfer the mixture to a shallow baking dish. Place it in the freezer.
3   After 30 minutes, check the mixture. If it has begun to freeze, remove from the freezer and scrape it with a fork to grate it up. Place it back in freezer and repeat until the whole mix is frozen and grated.
4   Serve with whipped cream (above) or vanilla ice cream.

olive oil cake, candied citrus, whipped cream
pg 216

lemon granita with whipped cream
pg 217

baked ricotta, stone fruit, honey
pg 222

affogato
pg 223

baked ricotta, stone fruit, honey

serves 4

This dessert is for the lover of the savory-sweet combo and who would look for a cheese course instead of dessert. Ricotta is definitely one of my top five favorite foods; I have been known to eat it plain on toast. The most important thing about this recipe is buying the right ricotta. Do not buy the regular grocery store variety. It is generally watery and doesn't have enough fat content to get the creaminess you're after. Take the time to seek out a more authentic artisanal variety, or go to your closest old-school Italian market to get the good stuff.

for the ricotta

2 tablespoons	olive oil
2 cups	ricotta cheese
	sea salt
20	grinds black pepper, coarse
1 teaspoon	chili flakes
1	whole lemon peel, pith removed
8	thyme sprigs

1   Preheat the oven to 375°F.
2   Grease four sections of a muffin tin with 1 tablespoon olive oil, draining off excess.
3   Divide the ricotta among the four sections and press down gently just to make sure they will hold together. Place the pan in the oven and bake until just set and the cheese can be removed without coming apart, approximately 15–17 minutes. Remove from the oven and allow to cool slightly.
4   Use a mini offset spatula or knife to gently separate the edges of the ricotta from the side of the molds. Place a sheet pan lined with parchment paper firmly against the muffin tin and carefully flip over so that the ricotta transfers to the sheet pan.
5   Drizzle the cheese with the remaining 1 tablespoon olive oil.
6   Season the cheese with sea salt, black pepper, and chili flakes. Top each with the pieces of lemon peel and thyme sprigs. Place the sheet pan back into the oven and bake until slightly golden brown around the edges, another 10–12 minutes

to serve

2	nectarines, plums, or peaches, cut into ½-inch-thick wedges
2 tablespoons	olive oil
	sea salt
4	portions baked ricotta
1 tablespoon	honey
2	sprigs thyme, leaves only
	zest of half a lemon

1   Place the fruit wedges in a bowl and dress with 1 tablespoon olive oil and season with sea salt.
2   Put each baked ricotta on an individual plate for serving and drizzle with the honey and remaining 1 tablespoon olive oil.
3   Top with the dressed fruit, thyme leaves, and lemon zest.

affogato

serves 4

The simplest of the simple desserts but one of the most craveable. In the case of dessert, affogato, the Italian word for "drowned," refers to ice cream swimming in a shot of perfect espresso. If you don't have an espresso machine you can substitute with strong regular coffee (though it won't be the same) or cold brew concentrate. Also, I have a confession to make: Häagen-Dazs is hands-down my favorite brand of ice cream. It is my guilty pleasure and it is what I use at home. There are only two ingredients in this dish, which means there is nothing to hide behind; subpar ice cream or coffee will ruin it. My suggestion is get your hands on some vanilla bean Häagen-Dazs and an espresso machine.

4 scoops vanilla ice cream or gelato
4 shots of espresso

1 Place one scoop of ice cream (or gelato) in a glass.
2 Pour the warm shot of espresso over the ice cream.
3 Be very happy.

piemontese style hot chocolate

makes 1 quart

Sometimes all you need after dinner is a little shot of chocolate. This is rich, satisfying, and easy to make. Taken from the traditions of the north of Italy, it certainly puts our little packets of Swiss Miss to shame. You can make this in a large batch and keep it in the refrigerator. Just reheat over a double boiler when you are ready to use it on those chilly nights when only a smooth cup of sipping chocolate will do. It's very rich, so it's best served in espresso cups rather than traditional mugs.

3 cups heavy cream
1 cup milk
½ cup sugar
pinch of salt
1 pound 70% bitter chocolate, chopped into small, even chunks

1 Place cream, milk, sugar, and salt in a saucepan and gently warm while stirring until the sugar is dissolved and the milk is hot. Be careful not to scorch it.
2 Place the chopped chocolate in a large heatproof bowl and pour the milk-cream mixture over. Let it sit for 5–10 minutes until the chocolate softens and melts. Whisk everything together until smooth.
3 Keep the hot chocolate in a double boiler or insulated carafe or pitcher to keep it warm.

toasted almond panna cotta

Panna cotta is the ideal dessert for non-bakers. Your friends and family will believe you are a phenomenal pastry chef when you present them with this silky sweet! I have always favored using the absolute minimum amount of gelatin in my *panna cotta*—just enough so that they will set. And because this translates into a looser, more delicate version, mine stays inside the ramekin, rather than being removed from the mold and turned out onto a plate as most *panna cottas* are. The almond and vanilla flavor combination in this recipe reminds me of the Good Humor toasted almond bar I used to get from the ice cream truck.

3 cups	whole raw almonds, plus ¼ cup chopped for garnish
2 cups	milk
5 cups	heavy cream
1	vanilla bean, split
1 cup	sugar
2	packets unflavored powdered gelatin or 6½ gelatin sheets honey

1   Heat the oven to 325°F. Place the almonds in an even layer on a sheet pan and place it in the oven. Toast until just golden, about 10 minutes.
2   Roughly chop the almonds, just to break them up.
3   Combine the milk, cream, vanilla bean, and chopped almonds in a large container with a lid or a mixing bowl covered with plastic wrap. Leave it to sit in the refrigerator overnight.
4   Transfer the cold vanilla-almond mixture to a small pot with the sugar and powdered gelatin. Let it sit for 5–10 minutes off heat, allowing the gelatin to bloom. Then place the pot on medium-low heat and warm it gently, whisking to dissolve the sugar and gelatin, being careful not to boil or burn the milk/cream. Once warm and the sugar and gelatin have completely dissolved, remove from the heat. (If you are using gelatin sheets, soak the gelatin in a bowl of cold water to soften as the milk warms. Squeeze the water out of the gelatin and whisk it into the warm milk and cream, until dissolved.)
5   Pass the whole mixture through a fine sieve over a large mixing bowl.
6   Divide equally among 6-ounce glasses, ramekins, or soufflé cups, and cover them tightly with plastic wrap. Place into the refrigerator to chill and set at least 4 hours.
7   Top with additional toasted chopped almonds and a drizzle of honey before serving.

summer berries, balsamic, black pepper, crème fraîche

serves 4

Berries in the height of summer should be eaten as naked as possible. And since they have been known to have disappeared completely by the time I walk home from the market, I always buy extra. This is great as a dessert but also works for breakfast because it's not very sweet. The balsamic and black pepper are just a slight enhancement to the berries, adding spice and acid to balance out the sweetness. And well, crème fraîche tastes good on anything.

6 cups	assorted berries (blue, black, black raspberries)
¼ cup	balsamic vinegar
½ cup	crème fraîche
	freshly cracked black pepper, coarse

1   Evenly divide the berries among four bowls and drizzle 1 tablespoon balsamic over the top of each.
2   Top each bowl with 2 tablespoons of crème fraîche and finish with 5 or 6 grinds of black pepper.

raspberry cream pie

I grew up devouring raspberries and cream with my dad; it has always been one of his favorite things to eat and he passed his love of this combo on to me. So it comes as no surprise that I would enjoy them in pie form as well. I don't consider myself a connoisseur of pies, but this recipe is inspired by one of the best pies I've ever eaten, that I tasted while visiting friends on the North Fork of Long Island. I'm not sure I can ever do it justice, but this is my best shot at getting to live that food memory over and over, without having to be on the North Fork. The original is with a more traditional pie crust, but I created an *amaretti* cookie crust instead. There is no better way to end a summer barbecue or picnic than this creamy delight.

for the crust

1½ cups	fine *amaretti* cookie crumbs
1½ tablespoons	sugar
½ teaspon	kosher salt
½ cup	melted butter
	cold butter for greasing the pie pan

1. Whisk the cookie crumbs, sugar, and salt together in a bowl.
2. Add the melted butter and use a wooden spoon or rubber spatula to mix until the crumbs are well coated.
3. Press the mixture into a slightly greased pie pan so that it is evenly distributed around the bottom and edges. Place in the refrigerator to chill until set.

for the cream filling

8 ounces	cream cheese
8 ounces	mascarpone
1 cup	confectioners' sugar
1 teaspoon	powdered gelatin (or 1 sheet of gelatin)
1½ cups	heavy cream whipped to soft peaks

1. Place the cream cheese, mascarpone, and sugar in a stand mixer with the beater attachment. Beat until fluffy.
2. Bloom the gelatin powder in 1½ tablespoons of cold water for 5 minutes. Add 1½ tablespoons of boiling water and stir to incorporate. (If using sheet gelatin, soften the gelatin in cold water. Squeeze out the excess water and dissolve the gelatin in ¼ cup hot water.)
3. Pour the bloomed gelatin into the cream mixture and beat gently on low just to incorporate.
4. Use a spatula or wooden spoon to gently fold the whipped cream into the sweetened cream and gelatin mixture.
5. Pour into the pie crust and spread in an even layer. Place in the fridge to chill and set; overnight is best.

for the raspberries

1 teaspoon powdered gelatin (or ½ sheet of gelatin)
2¾ cups raspberries
¾ cup sugar

1   Put the powdered gelatin in 1½ tablespoons of cold water to bloom.
    (If using sheet gelatin, place it in cold water to soften.)
2   Put the sugar and raspberries in a small saucepan with 1 teaspoon of water
    over low heat to warm, stirring occasionally. Cook until the sugar is dissolved
    and the raspberries begin to break down into a sauce, about 10 minutes.
3   Stir in the bloomed gelatin. (If using sheet gelatin, remove the gelatin from
    the water and squeeze out the extra water before transferring.) Remove
    from the heat and allow to cool completely.
4   When the pie is chilled, spread the cooled raspberry mixture over the top.
    Cut into slices and serve.

persimmon, honey, mascarpone crema   serves 4

Italians are amazing hosts. I was privileged to be invited to a rice farm and risotto
producer in the north of Italy, about 45 minutes away from the regal city of Torino, a
hidden gem amongst Italian cities. When I entered the dining room each morning,
I was presented with a single, super ripe persimmon (or *cachi*–"kaki"–as they are
called in Italy) on a plate. That was breakfast. (That and a cappuccino, of course.) It was
sweet and filling and odd and sort of perfect. In America, persimmons don't get the
credit they deserve and this dessert is a great way to showcase them, with the creamy
tanginess of mascarpone and a hint of sweet honey. Be careful when you choose
your persimmons–the fuyu variety, when very ripe, is the one you want. The other type,
hachiya, is chalky and makes your mouth feel funny if eaten raw.

for the mascarpone crema

1 cup mascarpone, at room temperature
½ cup cream, whipped to soft peaks

Gently fold the whipped cream into the mascarpone. Set aside.

for the finish

4 very ripe persimmons
½ cup mascarpone crema
2 tablespoons honey

1   Peel the persimmons and place each in a small bowl, topped with 2 tablespoons
    of the mascarpone crema and a drizzle of honey.

acknowledgments

This book is dedicated to my parents, Carol and David Robbins. For instilling the greatest love of hospitality and food, for always encouraging me to follow my career path, for providing an amazing educational foundation to achieve anything, and especially for not judging me, even at forty-two years old, when I announced I was going to quit my job and do nothing. Thank you for believing in me and having the unconditional confidence that I would find my way, even if I didn't.

Thanks also to:

Sondra Lender: There is no one more enthusiastic about my career or more supportive in my life. Thank you.

Gillian Blake: I believe you told me very firmly not to open a restaurant and write a book at the same time. Thank you for always giving me the most solid advice. I always hear you. I just don't always follow what you say. But you are always right.

Julia Jaksic: You are the best listener. Period. Thank you.

Laurie Saft: Thank you for always checking in, for always being there, for always putting a smile on my face and for years and years of friendship. And for taking a crazy trip to Italy with me to eat one meal.

Larissa Goldston: Thank you for our weekly coffee dates and for letting me vent to you for an hour at a time. I could not have made it through the past year without you.

Matt Robbins: Thank you for always being my very protective older brother and always saying the right thing when it counts most. I will always cherish our bagel mornings at Georgetown, our Tombs dinners on Dad, the memories of you getting sick at every meal in France, and the joys of eating asparagus with you in Italy.

Kari Stuart: Thank you for understanding my idea from our very first meeting. You were the first person to believe this book could happen and made sure that it did. Thanks for seeing me through the process and making sure I stayed on track. And mostly thank you for your wacky sense of humor.

Carrie King: Writer, therapist, and recipe tester all in one. Thank you, thank you, thank you. This book could have never happened without you and your incredible patience. Your enthusiasm for this book idea from the beginning, your ideas for how to execute it, and your constantly pushing me to make it better will never be forgotten. Thank you for getting the right words on to the page, for helping my voice be strong, and for always encouraging me to write the things I didn't always want to write. I could not have asked for a better writing partner in this endeavor.

Caitlin Leffel: Thank you for your passion for this project, for understanding what it was supposed to be and allowing me to do it my way (mostly), and for always fighting to keep the original vision both in writing and design intact.

Peter Ahlberg: I have strong ideas about design. Thank you for your amazing execution on them and constantly striving to get it just as I envisioned. It was great to go through this process and understand a completely new creative endeavor.

Evan Sung: Thank you for bringing my food to life on the page. Your vision is amazing and I am so honored to have gotten to work with you on this book.

Jesse Gerstein: Thank you for being a part of the team from the onset. And thank you for your believing in this book, before you had even seen it.

Keith Lender: Well...just because you asked.

Hillary Sterling: Thank you for a world of memories and for being an inspiration.

Eric Simpson: Thank you for making that phone call and saying you wanted to be by my side at Lilia. This book would not have happened without my trust in you to run the kitchen while I locked myself in my apartment to write so soon after we opened. Thank you for seamlessly making my presence felt even when I wasn't there. Thank you for pulling double duty during the photo shoot, for making a bunch a food you had never seen, and for helping with the Asian chapter so diligently. And mostly, thank you for making me laugh all day long, every day for the past sixteen months.

Eric Rentz: Thank you for sharing your knowledge of Asian cuisine with me unconditionally, and for making Lilia constantly keep moving so I could work on this project.

Kathy Walker: Thank you for all of your help in developing the dessert section of this book. It would not have happened without you

To the entire Lilia team: Thank you for your dedication to the restaurant, your enthusiasm, and for inspiring me daily to do what we do. Hopefully this book has given you a little glimpse into me and why I am who I am.

Sean Feeney: You are such a big part of this story. You watched so much of it happen, we shared so many of these meals together. Thank you for being my taste tester. Thank you for asking me to be your partner. Thank you for being my biggest fan. Thank you for being the partner I have always looked for. I could not have hoped for anyone better. Every day is not necessarily a good day, but thank you for wanting to believe they are and sharing that mantra with me over and over. And to Maria Feeney, thank you for so graciously sharing your husband with me.

Tony Mantuano: You are the best mentor ever. I could only think about you and Kathy writing your books as I delved into this journey day after day. Thank you for all of your support over the years, for instilling a love of Italian food and culture in me, and for set-ting such a positive example for me for the past fourteen years.

Lauren Barford: Thank you for introducing me to Pilates, and for your unbelievable patience in the teaching process. Mostly, thank you for becoming my friend over hours in the studio. I'm not sure there is anyone who saw my transformation more closely than you.

Todd Stein: Thank you for encouraging me to go on Weight Watchers. Our first conver-sation about it forever lives in my head. I will always think of it as a life-changing moment.

index

First published in the United States of
America in 2017 by:

Rizzoli International Publications, Inc.
300 Park Avenue South
New York, NY 10010
www.rizzoliusa.com

Copyright © Missy Robbins

ISBN: 978-0-8478-5997-9
Library of Congress Control Number:
2016956273

Distributed to the US Trade by
Random House, New York

All photographs by Evan Sung
Design: AHL&CO, Peter J. Ahlberg,
Kyle Chaille

2017 2018 2019 2020 / 10 9 8 7 6 5 4 3 2 1

Printed in China